I0819184

MOMENTS OF JOY

MOMENTS OF

90 DAYS OF ENCOURAGEMENT FOR PARENTS OF CHILDREN WITH SPECIAL NEEDS

CAMILLE JOY

WATERBROOK

WaterBrook

An imprint of the Penguin Random House Christian Publishing Group,
a division of Penguin Random House LLC

1745 Broadway, New York, NY 10019

waterbrookmultnomah.com
penguinrandomhouse.com

Hardcover ISBN 978-0-593-60308-6
Ebook ISBN 978-0-593-60309-3

The Cataloging-in-Publication Data is on file with the Library of Congress.

Printed in the United States of America

1st Printing

First Edition

The authorized representative in the EU for product safety and compliance is
Penguin Random House Ireland, Morrison Chambers, 32 Nassau Street,
Dublin D02 YH68, Ireland. https://eu-contact.penguin.ie

BOOKMAKING TEAM: Editor: Estee Zandee · Production editor: Jessica Choi · Managing editor: Julia Wallace · Production manager: Meghan O'Leary · Copy editor: Cara Iverson · Proofreaders: Tracey Moore, Marissa Earl

Book design by Jo Anne Metsch

For details on special quantity discounts for bulk purchases,
contact specialmarketscms@penguinrandomhouse.com.

To my husband, Marcus, and our beautiful family, whose love and support have been my anchor through every season of life. I love you! Thank you for always believing in me when I didn't believe in myself.

To all the parents, caregivers, and families raising children with special needs. This book is for you. May it remind you of your strength, your resilience, and the boundless love that fuels your journey.

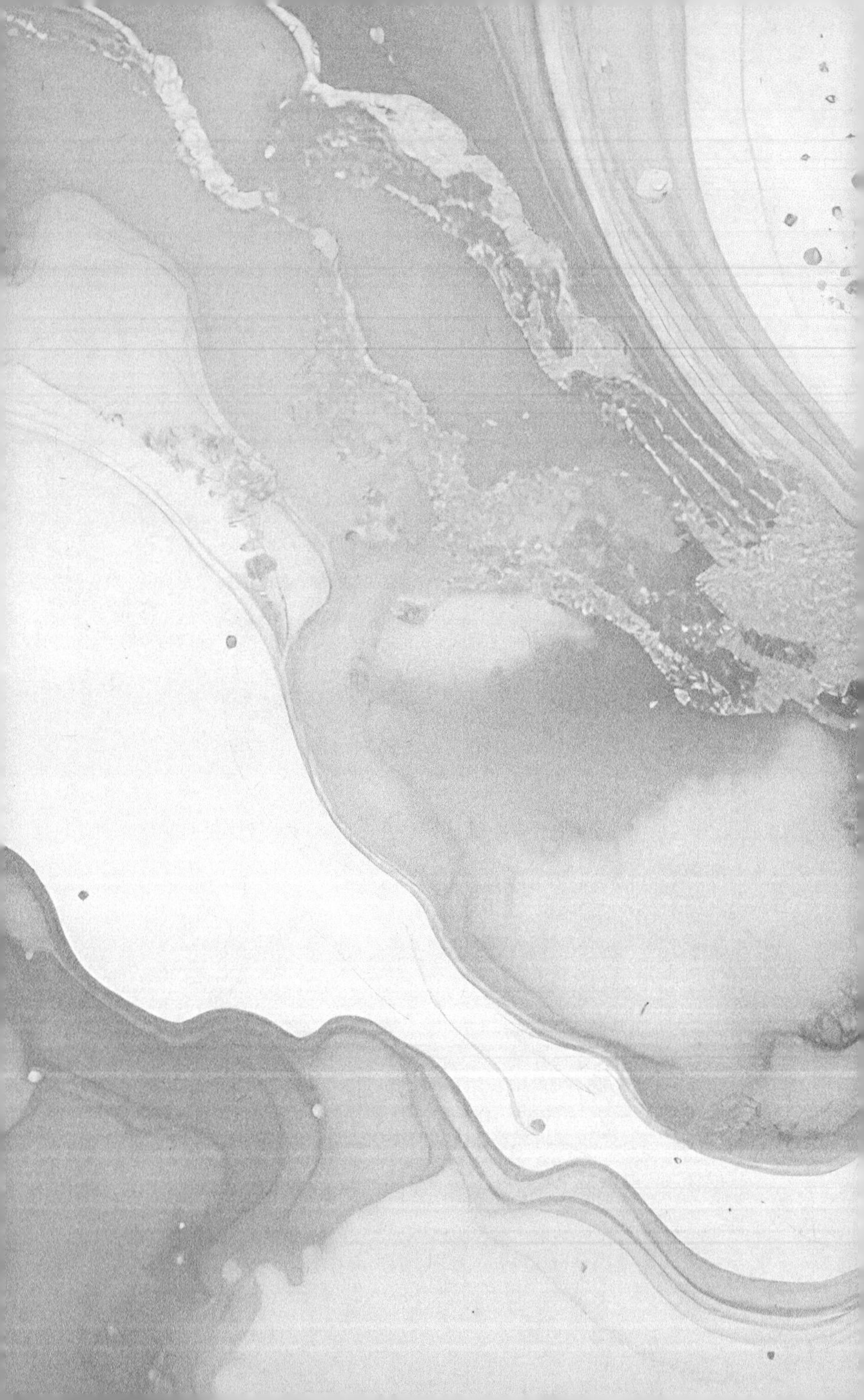

PREFACE

Dear Friend,

When my son Maison was born, the doctors told us he had several heart defects. I prayed fervently, asking others to join me in believing for a miracle—a normal heart. But his heart wasn't healed the way I had hoped. I remember the questions that flooded my mind: *Have I not been praying hard enough? Did I fail in some way? Is this my fault?* Those questions only grew louder when he was later diagnosed with autism, a new complication that was compounded by the ignorance and judgment of the outside world.

In my heartbreak and confusion, God showed me something extraordinary: My son was *perfect* just as he was. He reminded me that my child was created in His image, fearfully and wonderfully. Slowly, God helped me overcome the negative thoughts, the doubts, and the voices that tried to steal my joy. He gave me the strength to choose joy—every single day.

He will do the same for you.

If you're the parent of a special-needs child, you may

be feeling uncertain, overwhelmed, or frustrated. I want you to know that you don't have to go through it alone. I understand because I've walked this road too, but more importantly, Jesus understands. He sees you, hears your prayers, and walks alongside you, even on the hardest days. I pray that when you feel weary, unsure, or discouraged, the words in this devotional will give you strength, hope, and a reminder of the joy God offers even in the most challenging seasons.

Tag me at @momentsofjoypodcast as you read and post thoughts from this book. I'd love to know what's on your heart. There's a whole community of parents like us who truly get it. You are not alone.

With love and hope,
CAMILLE

MOMENTS OF JOY

1

I can do all this through him who gives me strength.

—*Philippians 4:13*

Receiving a diagnosis for your child can feel like a heavy blow. Fear, denial, and confusion may swirl in your mind. It's common to wonder if you're somehow to blame, but let me stop you there: You're not. The path forward isn't through debating blame; it's in looking for God at work.

I remember when my son was diagnosed with several heart defects before he was born. I was terrified. My mind raced with questions I didn't have answers to, and I felt completely unprepared for what was ahead. It was like stepping into a world I didn't know existed—one filled with surgeries, medical terms, ongoing specialist care, and so many unknowns. I wasn't just overwhelmed; I felt helpless and heartbroken, unsure how to be strong for a baby I hadn't even held yet. I knew so little about these challenges.

I'm telling you now what I wish I knew then: It's okay to feel a whirlwind of emotions. It's okay to mourn the picture of parenthood you had imagined. But let me tell you, that diagnosis doesn't mean defeat. It's a starting point for a new journey, one where you'll discover strengths you never knew you had.

For me, that diagnosis was a catalyst. It ignited a fire within me to become the best advocate for my child. I delved into research, learning everything I could about his condition and the resources available to us. I transformed into a warrior, determined to provide him with the best possible life.

So if you're facing a new diagnosis, challenges, or uncertainties, hang in there. You're stronger than you realize. Trust that God is with you. Remember, you're not just a parent; you're an advocate, a warrior, and a beacon of love for your child.

AFFIRMATION:

I am strong, capable, and filled with love.
God is with me on this path.

2

> You did not choose me, but I chose you and appointed you so that you might go and bear fruit—fruit that will last.
>
> —*John 15:16*

When we see other families walking an easier road, it's hard not to wonder if we were truly meant for this calling. *Why me?* we say to ourselves and ask in our more honest prayers.

But here's the truth: You were chosen. Not by chance, not by mistake, but intentionally chosen by God to love, nurture, and guide your child. He knew the challenges you would face, and He also knew the incredible strength, resilience, and love He placed within you to meet them.

God doesn't call the qualified; He qualifies the called. Every day that you show up, whether through small victories or hard-fought battles, you're bearing fruit that will last—fruit of love, patience, and faith. Your journey may not look like everyone else's, but it is uniquely purposeful and divinely appointed.

When the road feels heavy and doubt creeps in, remind yourself of this: God doesn't make mistakes. You were chosen to be your child's parent because no one else could do it better. Lean into the Father for wisdom, strength, and joy, and trust that His plan for you and your family is unfolding in ways greater than you can imagine.

AFFIRMATION:

I am chosen, equipped, and loved by God. He has called me to this journey, and with His strength, I can do all things.

3

LORD, be gracious to us;
we long for you.
Be our strength every morning,
our salvation in time of distress.
—*Isaiah 33:2*

While I was pregnant with my youngest son, Maison, I already had four boys and a total of sixteen years of parenting experience. I thought I knew everything there was to know about being a mom and raising children.

That was until I gave birth to a child in a separate category. Parenting a child with special needs is very different from raising a typical one. There have been times I felt like I was in the twilight zone. Day after day, we go through the same routine, not knowing if things will ever change. We don't know if the expected milestones will ever be reached. With typical children, we can be certain there is an expiration date for certain behavior, but with special-needs ones, that's not necessarily the case.

I've learned I can't walk the journey of being a special-needs parent in my own strength. And, thankfully, I don't have to. I've realized I don't need to have it all figured out.

Friend, God wants us to lean on Him. Even in parenting. Especially in parenting. And that's what I decided to do. This means recognizing in the hardest moments that He is present, guiding and sustaining us. I lean on Him when the weight of advocacy feels too heavy, when exhaustion sets in, or when I fear for my child's future. Leaning on God looks like whispered prayers in the night when I'm so exhausted, trusting that He hears and cares. It looks like recalling Scripture and holding on to its truths. Leaning on Him is remembering that it's okay that I don't have all the answers, because He does. We lean on God when we find comfort in His promises in the times we feel alone and when we hold on to faith in the times it seems nobody understands.

In our moments of weakness, we can experience His strength in profound ways. His power is made perfect in our weakness.

AFFIRMATION:

In my moments of weakness, I will not forget to lean on Christ. His grace is sufficient for me.

4

> The peace of God, which transcends all understanding, will guard your hearts and your minds in Christ Jesus.
>
> —*Philippians 4:7*

The other day, as I sat on my bed, I experienced one of those rare moments when I felt filled with an unexpected sense of peace. It was as if all the weight of the world had been lifted from my shoulders, if only for a fleeting moment.

It's easy to get caught up in the never-ending cycle of appointments, therapies, and to-do lists, but it's essential to pause, rest for a minute, and embrace the beauty that surrounds us. It's in those quiet moments that we find solace and strength to carry on. As parents, we often put immense pressure on ourselves to be everything for our children: caregivers, advocates, therapists, and so much more. But it's crucial to remember that we're human and it's okay to recharge our own batteries.

So, friend, I urge you to seek out those moments of peace, however short-lived they may be. Whether it's a quiet moment alone, a walk in nature, or simply sitting on your bed, embrace it fully. Sometimes I find peace by stepping outside and feeling the breeze on my face, brewing a cup of tea, or opening my Bible to a favorite verse.

The activity doesn't have to be long or elaborate; it just has to be real. Allow yourself to let go of the worries and fears that weigh you down, and bask in the beauty of the present moment.

And when the chaos returns, as it always does, hold on to the memory of that peace. Let it be a guiding light that sustains you through the storms and reminds you of the immense love and strength that reside within you.

AFFIRMATION:

In the midst of chaos, I will seek God's peace.

5

> Above all else, guard your heart,
> for everything you do flows from it.
> —*Proverbs 4:23*

I got a phone call from a member of my extended family a while ago. She called to tell me that I needed to be potty training my son, and she gave me firm directions on how to do it.

I reminded her that Maison is my fifth child and that I potty trained four children before him. I gave her a little education on autistic children and hung up. I was very annoyed. She apologized in a text right after, but the damage was done.

To any parent raising a special-needs child who is over the typical age of potty training and other milestones, don't you dare hang your head or be embarrassed. People are often well meaning, but they don't know what you're experiencing. No one else knows your child's specific needs as well as you do.

You have not failed to do your job as a parent just because your child doesn't match the image of what someone else imagines to be "correct." Every child moves at the pace that's just right for them, and that pace is not a mistake. God knows your child intimately. He created them, He loves them, and He's guiding their journey in His perfect timing. Trust that and stand confidently in the path He has for both of you.

AFFIRMATION:
I am proud of my child's development and all God is doing in our lives.

6

The LORD is close to the brokenhearted
and saves those who are crushed in spirit.
—*Psalm 34:18*

Have you ever felt like you wanted to have a meltdown after you finished consoling your child who was having a meltdown of their own?

It's tough! But you are not alone. Your feelings are valid. I have struggled with anxiety and thoughts of hopelessness during those moments. I know this journey can be very isolating. And unlike most other parts of parenting, you can't always pick up the phone and call a friend who gets it, because not everyone does.

The exhaustion, the emotional weight, and the energy drain after pouring everything you have into helping your child regulate are hard to explain to those who haven't lived it.

It's in these moments—when our strength feels depleted and our patience runs thin—that we need to remember that we are not in this alone. God is not watching from a distance. He is near. His presence isn't just a comforting thought; it is a real, active source of strength. He sees the tears we cry after we finally get our child to sleep. He understands the weight we carry, the unspoken prayers, the silent pleas for just a little more endurance. And He meets us there.

When we remember that God is with us, the load doesn't disappear, but our perspective shifts. We're reminded that we're not carrying this weight on our own. We don't need to have it all figured out. We can rest in the assurance that the same God who designed our children, with all their unique needs, also equipped us to be their parents.

So, in your hardest moments, breathe. Let the tears flow if they need to. You are not failing. You are not alone. You've been built for this, and God is walking the path with you, every single step of the way.

AFFIRMATION:

God is near. I am never alone.

7

> He who began a good work in you will carry it on to completion until the day of Christ Jesus.
>
> —*Philippians 1:6*

I remember in first grade planting seeds in a little Styrofoam cup at school and bringing it home to sit on the windowsill. Every day, I'd check it, eager to see the seeds sprout. The joy that came when a tiny leaf finally pushed up through the soil was indescribable. From that moment, I learned something important: There is beauty in the process. The act of planting a seed with hope teaches us about patience, trust, and the surety of something good coming.

We nurture, care for, and pour our hearts into our children, all while hoping and praying for beautiful outcomes. But unlike with the seeds in the cup, the process with our children can feel less certain. We don't always know if growth is coming or when it might appear, and that unknown weighs heavily.

Yet just as with that tiny seed, there is beauty in the process—God's process. Philippians 1:6 assures us that He is at work and is actively nurturing, guiding, and shaping us and our children through every challenge and triumph.

God is in control. Our precious children are even more

precious to Him, as He sees the potential in them that we may not always see. When we trust Him, it lifts the weight of controlling the end result off our shoulders. God is guiding the process and will bring it to completion in His perfect timing.

Ask God to show you signs of His work throughout the day. He's bringing about beautiful things.

AFFIRMATION:

I rest in the assurance that God will bring to completion the good work He has started. Beauty is unfolding in His perfect timing.

8

I have told you these things so that you will be filled with my joy. Yes, your joy will overflow!

—*John 15:11*, NLT

While raising my son with special needs, I often feel lost and overwhelmed. It seems like there is no road map, no one to turn to for guidance. Nights are sleepless. Days are filled with meltdowns. The weight of advocacy can feel unbearably heavy and dark.

But during one of the hardest moments, I made a choice. Instead of letting despair take over, I made a promise to myself that I would hold on to something brighter: I chose joy. It wasn't easy and didn't come naturally every time, but I refused to let darkness win. And it's made an incredible difference.

Being a parent to a child with special needs isn't about perfection; it's about embracing the messy, challenging journey and finding beauty in it all. Yes, it's hard. There are moments when joy feels out of reach, buried under layers of exhaustion and doubt.

Choosing to hold on to joy is about finding peace and hope in chaos. For me, that comes from my faith and knowing I'm never alone in this journey. God promised us joy.

So, today and every day, I make a conscious decision to choose joy. Despite the struggles, despite the uncertainty, I hold on to the truth that there's always something to be grateful for and always something to smile about. Sometimes it's the sound of Maison's laughter echoing down the hallway or a quiet moment with a cup of coffee before the rest of the family wakes up. It's watching my son flap his hands with excitement or seeing him reach for a favorite toy. It's the warm sun on my face in the car-pool line or a hug from one of my older children after a long day. These are the little joys that remind me that God is near and life is beautiful.

No matter how tough things get, we always have the power to choose what we focus on. I invite you to join me in the choice to embrace joy whenever possible. Make a declaration today that despite how you feel and what may be going on around you, you will choose joy.

AFFIRMATION:

Today, I choose joy and find strength and comfort in God's presence.

9

Come to me, all who labor and are heavy laden, and I will give you rest.

—*Matthew 11:28*, ESV

There will be days when the weight of everything feels too much to bear. You haven't slept in days, resources seem nonexistent, and advocating for your child feels like battling a giant. In those moments, the dam breaks and tears fall freely. Don't push them away. Crying is not a sign of weakness; it's a sign of a heart that deeply cares.

Jesus wept too. He cried at the tomb of Lazarus (see John 11:35), and He wept over Jerusalem (see Luke 19:41). In the Garden of Gethsemane, He poured out His soul in anguish. If the Son of God had moments when tears were His language, then we can know that our tears are not shameful; they are sacred. Psalm 56:8 tells us that God keeps track of all our sorrows and collects our tears in a bottle. He sees every one.

We watch movies where superheroes tirelessly save the day, but the reality of raising a child with special needs is far from a comic book. It's a messy, emotional journey filled with exhaustion, frustration, and, yes, even tears. But here's the secret: Your tears are a testament to your deep, unwavering love and fierce advocacy for your child.

Remember this:

- You are not alone. Countless parents understand this struggle.
- Your tears don't diminish your strength; they show your humanity.
- Crying can be a release—a way to cleanse and find renewed resolve.
- There is help available. Don't be afraid to reach out for support.

Take a deep breath, let the tears flow, and know that tomorrow is a new day.

AFFIRMATION:

My tears are a sign of my love,
and they will not weaken me.

10

Do not fear, for I am with you;
do not be dismayed, for I am your God.
I will strengthen you and help you;
I will uphold you with my righteous right hand.
—*Isaiah 41:10*

I didn't realize how much I needed help until I felt overwhelmed and lost. There was a season when I felt like I had no one who truly understood what I was going through. Dealing with the public school system for my son's special-education needs nearly broke me. I discovered that his school wasn't following the law when it came to his individualized education plan (IEP), and suddenly it was up to me to learn the laws, speak up, and hold the school accountable. I sat alone late at night, exhausted from emails and research, wondering why this fight had to be so hard.

Many parents suffer silently, afraid to ask for help for fear of being judged or seen as weak. But we're not alone in this struggle. I recently talked with a group of other moms of special-needs kids, and so many of them also felt misunderstood, alone, and burdened. Some shared how they stopped attending family gatherings because the stares and unsolicited advice became too much. Others admitted they cried after dropping their kids off, unsure of how they'd make it through the week. It broke my heart to hear so many stories that mirrored my own: of parents stretched thin, carrying more than anyone realizes, and feeling invisible in it all.

Asking for help is not a sign of weakness; it's a sign of strength and courage. Whether what you need is professional assistance, community services, or mental health support, getting the resources you need will help you and your family thrive. We're all in this together, and there are countless resources available to lighten our load, like in that famous scene in the movie *Mrs. Doubtfire* when the nanny is running to help someone choking and yells, "Help is on the way, dear!" Please do yourself a favor and request the assistance. Somewhere along the way, many of us started believing that struggling alone somehow makes us stronger or more faithful. But we don't get extra points for doing everything the hard way. God designed us for community, support, and grace. Asking for help isn't weakness; it's wisdom.

God is compassionate and wants us to invite Him in to help. So if you don't know where to start, try prayer. Invite Him into the mess—He's ready to help.

AFFIRMATION:

I am brave and strong for seeking assistance when I need it. Help is always within reach.

11

Your labor is not in vain.

—1 Corinthians 15:58, NKJV

Today, I sat in an IEP meeting for my son. These meetings are never easy, but this one was particularly heavy. I spoke up about how excluded the children in special education are from the rest of the school. They don't have music, art, or gym—the very subjects that help children explore creativity, move their bodies, and connect with peers. Their school experience feels so limited and isolating.

By the end of the meeting, there were many tears—not because immediate change was guaranteed but because sharing our truth opened eyes and hearts. Sometimes the systems we're up against are too big to move, too ingrained to shift overnight. But even when it seems that nothing has changed, we're planting seeds—seeds of awareness, seeds of compassion, and seeds of change for the children who will come after ours.

Advocating isn't easy. It's exhausting, and it often feels like we're shouting into the void. But we must hold on to hope that the small ripples we create will grow into waves of change. We may not see the harvest, but the seeds we sow today could lead to a brighter future for another child tomorrow.

Let's keep pressing forward, knowing that every word spoken, every meeting attended, and every tear shed has the power to create change not just for our children but for others' children too.

AFFIRMATION:

I am planting seeds of hope and change, trusting that God will bring growth in His time.

12

> Rejoice always, pray continually, give thanks in all circumstances; for this is God's will for you in Christ Jesus.
>
> —*1 Thessalonians 5:16–18*

My son has been enjoying watching YouTube and learning about different fruits. One day while sitting on the couch, he said, "Watermelon, grapefruit, strawberry!" I turned and said, "Wow, Maison! You sure are speaking a lot today!" He jumped up in joy and ran over to me. He began to say the words *orange, grape, peach, kiwi, blueberry,* and *dragon fruit*! I was blown away, and we both smiled from ear to ear in total excitement. I could tell that his little heart was filled with joy at seeing how his words made me happy. I was so excited because Maison is non-verbal and doesn't speak much on his own.

As parents raising children with special needs, we live with a lot of uncertainty. There are moments when we have doubts about the future—what it will look like for our kids and how we'll navigate all the coming challenges. We have breakdowns at times because the pressure to advocate and always make the right decision can be so great. Don't make permanent homes of those uncertainties and doubts. Give yourself permission to celebrate. Let yourself smile and feel those positive emotions. Every good thing—however small or big—is worth rejoicing in.

Scripture encourages us to rejoice, pray, and give thanks in all circumstances. This can be challenging, but it's in these moments of gratitude that we find strength. Every glimpse of goodness reflects God's hand at work in our lives and in the lives of our children. Hold on to these glimpses of joy as reminders of the incredible love and resilience that exist within your family.

AFFIRMATION:

I give myself permission to celebrate every single little milestone.

13

The LORD does not look at the things people look at. People look at the outward appearance, but the LORD looks at the heart.

—*1 Samuel 16:7*

Comparison affects us all. It's very easy to fall into the trap of holding up your child's milestones to those of other children. Having four typical children before Maison gave me expectations that I often need to reevaluate. As he grows and his speech develops, I've had to slow down and learn to celebrate his unique pace of growth.

Your journey is yours alone. It's full of both challenges and victories that are unique to you and your child. Constantly measuring ourselves and our children against others only steals the joy in our own progress.

We compare with others in hopes of finding validation, yet really comparison makes us feel inadequate and leads to self-doubt. But you know your child, your family's needs, your goals the best. You know more than you think you do, and you are doing better than you imagine. Friend, the path you walk with your child is one of a kind. Walk it with confidence.

AFFIRMATION:

I am proud of our unique journey. I release the urge to compare myself to others and instead embrace the joy found in the progress my child and I have made.

14

Weeping may stay for the night,
but rejoicing comes in the morning.
—*Psalm 30:5*

One night at the hospital years ago, we heard the constant beeping of machines in the pediatric intensive care unit. It's a sound we had grown accustomed to, signaling how our child's vital signs were doing. After Maison's third heart surgery, the beeping seemed louder than ever. When he woke up, he cried for hours despite the pain medicine. I felt overwhelmed, close to breaking down, but my husband's words snapped me back to reality. He reminded me that the pain wouldn't last forever and joy would come in the morning, just like the psalm says.

"Camille, you can't fall apart now." His voice was a gentle anchor during the chaos, and his reminder pulled me out of despair. The darkness of the night, the anguish in Maison's cries, would not endure. With each day, there is a fresh promise of joy. And in that promise, we find the strength to persevere, to weather the storms that life brings.

In the darkest moments, when the weight of our burdens threatens to overwhelm us, we find solace in the reassurance that the worst moments, longest nights, and harshest pain won't last forever. Joy will return.

And each night we've weathered brings us that much closer to sunrise. Face each night with courage, because the challenges you face are stepping stones to brighter days.

AFFIRMATION:

I am strong enough to endure the night.

15

> God has not given us a spirit of fear, but of power and of love and of a sound mind.
>
> —*2 Timothy 1:7*, NKJV

The other day, something as simple as getting out of the car made me pause and think. I noticed that Maison didn't know how to open the car door by himself. It struck me that there are many little things I do for him every day, things that most parents of typical children may take for granted.

This realization brought a new worry into my heart. I started to fear all the potential emergencies that could arise and how Maison might not even recognize them as emergencies, let alone know how to respond. But I took a deep breath and reminded myself not to let fear consume me. Instead, I made a quiet decision to start teaching my son one small thing at a time. That day, we practiced unlocking the door together, step-by-step. It didn't go perfectly, but it was a start. Fear didn't get the final word; action did.

Fear might knock on our doors, but faith answers with courage. I want to remind you that we are equipped with a spirit of power, love, and a sound mind. This enables us to face challenges with resilience and trust in God's protection for our families.

It's okay to feel afraid sometimes—it's a natural part of the journey. But fear doesn't define our abilities as parents. Let's embrace our fears as invitations for growth and strength.

AFFIRMATION:

Fear is an invitation to grow. I can overcome any obstacle that comes my way.

16

We can make our plans,
but the LORD determines our steps.
—*Proverbs 16:9*, NLT

Life often throws us unexpected curveballs. The other morning, I woke up to find Maison feeling sick. Instead of carrying on with my agenda, I chose to stay home and give him the care and support he needed.

In these moments, flexibility becomes our ally, allowing us to navigate challenges with grace and resilience. We're no strangers to unpredictability. Our days are shaped by the ever-changing needs of our children, requiring us to adapt and prioritize their well-being over our own plans. And although these interruptions can feel inconvenient, they're also sacred invitations to love our children deeply—through presence, patience, and quiet sacrifice. Every detour is a chance to choose love over control, compassion over productivity. That morning reminded me that sometimes the most important thing God will ever call us to do is simply be there for our kids.

Sitting beside Maison, I was reminded of the privilege and responsibility of parenting a child with special needs. It's a journey marked by joy and sacrifice, victories and setbacks. But through it all, love and presence guide us forward.

AFFIRMATION:

I embrace the unexpected with grace, knowing that each detour is an opportunity to love my child.

17

> Do not forget this one thing, dear friends: With the LORD a day is like a thousand years, and a thousand years are like a day.
>
> —*2 Peter 3:8*

For years, I cried because Maison wouldn't sleep through the night. Six years to be exact. Sleep deprivation has affected my mental health at times. There have been days when he would stay up all night. For most parents, being up all night is only a thing of the newborn days, yet that's not the case for many of us parents of kids with special needs.

But I have great news. My son now sleeps through the night. I had the random idea to let Maison fall asleep in my bed and then transfer him when he was asleep. I repeated the action for another night. Then another.

I can't take credit for this miracle. God gave me a solution and it worked. We are going on one month of Maison sleeping in his own bed. At the end of the day, it wasn't a specialized bed that was the answer. It wasn't therapy. It was God. He answers prayers.

Waiting for answers can be one of the most challenging aspects of this journey. We yearn for progress and solutions, but they seem to elude us. In 2 Peter 3:8, we are reminded that with God, time takes on a different dimension. What feels like waiting or stagnation to us may actually be part of His perfect plan and timing. His timeline is beyond our understanding, and even when we don't see immediate results, He's still working.

When nothing works, I get on my knees and pray. When I can't do it, God can.

Maison may have special needs, but he also has a loving and powerful God—a God who sees every challenge, walks with him through every struggle, and has a purpose for his life.

AFFIRMATION:

I will stay encouraged while I wait.
God knows what we need.

18

Even to your old age and gray hairs
I am he, I am he who will sustain you.
I have made you and I will carry you;
I will sustain you and I will rescue you.
—*Isaiah 46:4*

Sometimes we hear someone say, "We made it out of the trenches," and we celebrate with them. But what if you're still entrenched in overwhelming challenges? What if each day feels like a battle, with hospital visits, prayers for your child's very life, and a constant struggle to maintain your own mental and emotional well-being?

It's okay to acknowledge these struggles, to allow yourself to feel the weight of it all. Scripture reminds us of God's promise to never leave us or forsake us. Even when it feels like you're lost in the trenches, God is right there with you, offering comfort and strength beyond measure. He understands your pain, your fears, and your doubts, and He longs to carry you through the darkest moments.

When you're at your lowest, when the tears won't stop flowing, when anxiety is high and depression is keeping you low, I encourage you to turn to God in prayer. Pour out your heart to Him as honestly as you can, knowing that He cares for you more deeply than anyone else ever could. Let His presence surround you like a warm embrace, reminding you that you are never alone.

Although we may not always see the physical healing or growth we long for in our children, we can trust in the promise of God's unfailing love and His eternal presence. He sees every tear you shed, hears every prayer you utter, and holds you close in the palm of His hand.

As you navigate the challenges of raising children with disabilities and special needs, remember that you are stronger than you know, braver than you feel, and deeply loved by a God who will never let you go.

AFFIRMATION:

God has sustained me this far,
and He will sustain me forever.

19

Cast your burden on the LORD,
and he will sustain you;
he will never permit
the righteous to be moved.
—*Psalm 55:22,* ESV

Today, my husband and I made the difficult decision to entrust Maison to the care of a babysitter for the day so we could spend quality time with our older children. It marked our first time leaving him alone with her, a step filled with apprehension and uncertainty.

Our lives often revolve around Maison's needs, prioritizing his well-being above all else, yet we know how important it is to nurture our relationships with our other children. It was time they had our undivided attention. We planned a quick trip to see a rodeo. Maison would've become overstimulated in the crowded place.

Throughout the day, I found myself frequently checking the home cameras, consumed by anxiety over leaving him in another's care. However, as the day unfolded, I was able to relax since our older children had so much fun with rides, games, and shows, soaking in every experience with delight. We laughed, adventured, and cherished memories together. The day was brimming with joy and delicious food, a testament to the importance of nurturing familial bonds. And Maison had a great day with his babysitter.

Stepping away from the familiar routine and prioritizing our own well-being required courage, yet in doing so, we affirmed our worth as individuals and as a family. We reminded ourselves that our needs matter too—that rest, joy, and connection are not luxuries but rather are necessary parts of a healthy, thriving life together.

I find solace in the words of Psalm 55, a beautiful reminder that by entrusting our cares to the divine, we find everything we need.

By nurturing our well-being, we are better able to show up with presence and joy as a caregiving parent.

AFFIRMATION:

By taking care of myself, I am better able to care for my family.

20

> Do not despise these small beginnings, for the LORD rejoices to see the work begin.
>
> —*Zechariah 4:10*, NLT

"I go potty," six-year-old Maison told me one day after he used the bathroom. I never thought I would rejoice over poop. I had spent about three years potty training him, obsessed with trying to reach a typical milestone. Then his behavior analysis therapist said, "Mom, let's pause." I had forgotten to appreciate our unique pace.

Progress is not always linear, and growth comes in many forms. Potty training may seem like a normal accomplishment to some, but to us, it's a triumph that represents years of patience, dedication, and love.

As parents raising a child with special needs, we witness miracles every day: in the smile that lights up our child's face, in the sound of their laughter, and, yes, even in the words "I go potty." These moments remind us of the grace that surrounds us, the strength that sustains us, and the love that fills our hearts.

Progress may happen in fits and starts; you may see growth in minutes or over years of practice. But don't grow disheartened. Instead, pace yourself to your child's timing and celebrate every small victory along the way.

AFFIRMATION:

I embrace each step of the journey with love, faith, and gratitude, knowing that with God's strength, I am enough and so is my love.

21

> What God has joined together, let no one separate.
>
> —*Mark 10:9*

Raising a child with disabilities can place unique pressures on a relationship. The emotional weight, constant advocacy, and unpredictable routines often leave little time for connection between spouses. But if you give your relationship intentionality and care, it doesn't have to fade into the background; it can grow stronger, more compassionate, and more deeply rooted in love.

Here are four practical tips to help you carve out time for each other and strengthen your bond:

1. **Make time for regular dates.** Set aside regular time—monthly, weekly, or whenever works best for your schedule—to connect without distractions. This could mean dinner at your favorite restaurant, a walk in the park, or even watching a movie together after the kids are in bed. And when leaving the house isn't possible, get creative with day dates at home: a backyard picnic, cooking a new recipe together, or a relaxing do-it-yourself spa day. The goal isn't perfection; it's connection.
2. **Utilize respite care.** Don't hesitate to seek help from trusted family members, friends, or respite services to

take care of your children while the two of you spend time together. It helps you recharge and reconnect as a couple.

3. **Communicate openly.** Share your honest feelings, concerns, needs, and joys with each other. Honest communication doesn't mean unloading every frustration in the heat of the moment; it means creating space for both people to be heard, seen, and understood. Aim to speak with love and listen with grace, remembering that you're on the same team.
4. **Prioritize self-care.** Remember to take care of yourselves individually as well. Nurture your physical, emotional, and spiritual well-being so you can show up fully for your spouse and children.

Lean on each other and lean on your faith. A strong marriage doesn't just help you survive the hard days; it becomes a sacred space where God's peace dwells and His love is made visible. So, as you invest in each other, trust that you are also making room for Him to move, heal, and draw you ever closer—not only to each other but also to Him.

AFFIRMATION:

As partners, we support and cherish each other through every high and low. Together, we can overcome anything.

22

> Trust in the LORD with all your heart
> and lean not on your own understanding;
> in all your ways submit to him,
> and he will make your paths straight.
> —*Proverbs 3:5–6*

Letting someone else care for our children can feel overwhelming. I know the fear and hesitation because I've lived it. My son Maison has autism, intellectual disability, and congenital heart disease, and his needs are complex. For a long time, I believed I had to be everything for him. The thought of someone else stepping in filled me with anxiety. What if they didn't understand him? What if they made a mistake?

But over time, I learned something important: Trying to carry it all on my own wasn't good for me or Maison. I wasn't thriving. I was tired, stretched thin, and losing pieces of myself. Eventually, I realized accepting help didn't mean I was failing. It was wise. It meant I was choosing to show up as the best version of myself, not the most exhausted one.

Letting others carry some of the responsibility took courage. I had to learn to trust that they could take care of Maison well, even if their care looked slightly different from mine. Friends and family members had other ideas and instincts, yet I saw how they loved Maison and expanded his world in beautiful ways. Proverbs 3:5–6 reminded me that my own understanding wasn't going to lead me where I needed to go. Trusting God meant trusting the support He placed around me, whether it was a family member, a teacher, or a kind stranger. As I slowly opened up to receive help, I found relief, new energy, and unexpected joy.

It's okay to lean on trusted people to help and support you. God never meant for you to walk this road alone. In fact, His plan for you includes rest and renewal given by others.

AFFIRMATION:

I can rely on God and trusted people to help me care for my child. His plan for me includes rest.

23

"I know the plans I have for you," declares the LORD, "plans to prosper you and not to harm you, plans to give you hope and a future."

—*Jeremiah 29:11*

We paint a picture in our minds of what our children's lives will be: filled with milestones like attending prom, walking across a graduation stage, leaving for college, getting married, and stepping into a promising career. We imagine birthday parties with friends, spontaneous road trips with siblings, and cheering from the sidelines at soccer games. But sometimes reality takes a different path. And with that divergence comes grief—not because we lack love but because we must release the picture we had painted and face the fears we never saw coming.

However, grief isn't a onetime event; it comes in waves. There are seasons when it crashes down unexpectedly—when we hear words we weren't prepared for or when a child the same age as ours hits milestones we're still waiting on. But as the waves come and go, we begin to discover the deep, beautiful truth: Our child is not broken; they are beautifully and wonderfully made.

We see that incredible beauty in the way our child remembers every birthday in the family or how they make us laugh with their unfiltered honesty. Maybe they don't speak much, but the way they light up when they hear music is pure joy. Perhaps they're a walking encyclopedia about trains or animals or outer space. Even if our child is nonverbal, there is beauty in every hum and excitement in every self-stimulatory behavior. One of my cousins has Down syndrome and autism, and she is the heart of our family. Her love for babies and old family photographs has made her the family historian, the hugger in chief, and the one who reminds us of the moments that truly matter.

Sometimes it's the world that needs to adjust its view of success. Not every life has to follow the traditional path. Some of the happiest and most impactful people never went to college or followed a straight line. Letting go of one dream often allows room for something truer, more fulfilling, and uniquely beautiful.

Jeremiah 29:11 reminds us that God's plans for our children are filled with hope, even when the road looks different than we expected. As we trust His vision, we will see that our special-needs child's future—though unique—is full of purpose, promise, and beauty.

AFFIRMATION:

I release the "perfect" picture and embrace the unique beauty of who my child is. I trust in God's perfect plans for their future.

24

"Neither this man nor his parents sinned," said Jesus, "but this happened so that the works of God might be displayed in him."

—*John 9:3*

When Maison was diagnosed with autism, I was desperately looking for a reason or cause. Was it something I did during pregnancy? Was it related to his heart surgery? The questions were endless and the answers difficult to find. But despite the chaos in my thoughts, I realized there was nothing I could have done differently to change things.

It's easy to fall into the trap of self-blame—question every decision, action, and moment and wonder if we could have somehow altered the course of our child's diagnosis. We carry the weight of guilt on our shoulders. But let me tell you something important: Your child's condition is not your fault. Your child's diagnosis is not a result of your actions or inactions. It is not a punishment for something you did or didn't do. It is simply a part of their journey and yours.

God has entrusted you with a special child. He knows your strength, your resilience, and your unwavering love. He has a good plan for your child and celebrates their intrinsic value. So, let go of the burden of guilt. Carrying that unnecessary weight around isn't helping you. Instead, start to pay attention to the beauty right where you are.

AFFIRMATION:

I release myself from guilt. I am a loving and capable parent, entrusted with a special child by a loving God.

25

> Faith is the substance of things hoped for, the evidence of things not seen.
>
> —*Hebrews 11:1*, NKJV

February 22, 2022, is etched in my heart as a memory that will never fade. It was the day my nonverbal son—the fifth blessing in our family—gazed into my eyes and whispered, "Mommy, I love you."

Four and a half years I waited for those precious words. I wondered if I would ever hear them.

I have four children who have no disabilities, and I've taken so much for granted. I used to get tired of hearing "Mommy" over and over, but with Maison, I knew what it was to go years without that word. I now celebrate this simple yet remarkable exchange on another level.

Hope is often underestimated, but it holds a power beyond comprehension. It's the flicker of light in the darkest nights and the longest waits. Hope sustains when nothing else remains.

Hope isn't merely wishful thinking; it's an expectation, a belief in unseen possibilities. Hope never gives up.

We don't know how or when our longings will be fulfilled, but we keep daring to hope for the big things and little things. Love on your babies tonight and celebrate them. Hope for them. Remember how far they've come.

AFFIRMATION:

I will keep hope alive. My child is spectacular!

26

> Let not your hearts be troubled. Believe in God; believe also in me.
>
> —*John 14:1*, ESV

There was a time when my husband and I shared a single car amid the hustle of managing the athletic and academic schedules of five kids, maintaining a household, and running our own businesses. With countless obligations, it would have been easy to succumb to frustration and discontentment. But instead, I made a conscious decision to shift my perspective: I chose gratitude.

I thanked God for the reliable car we did have—the vehicle that faithfully transported us from one destination to another. I thanked Him for the thriving businesses we owned and the blessing of our children, who were flourishing despite life's challenges. In counting my blessings, I found a new kind of peace and contentment. Choosing to be grateful helped me stop focusing on what was stressful and start seeing what was good.

Even when the schedules were packed and the days long, I reminded myself that God was still making a way. Gratitude didn't take the busy away, but it helped me handle it better. It made me more patient when I needed to fight for resources or felt unheard during my son's IEP meetings, allowed me to find strength when Maison was in the hospital for yet another surgery, and helped me combat the feelings of anxiety that come with caregiving. It gave me what I needed to keep going and enabled me to slow down, breathe, and remember that even this season had beauty.

Instead of dwelling on what you lack or the obstacles in your path, take a moment to reflect on the abundance that surrounds you. Find beauty in the small moments and joy in the simplest of blessings.

May gratitude become the melody of your heart and reveal the infinite grace and goodness of God.

AFFIRMATION:

I am thankful for the blessings that fill my life, both big and small.

27

There is a time for everything,
and a season for every activity under the heavens.
—*Ecclesiastes 3:1*

During a fall trip to Connecticut, I found myself driving along the highway, captivated by the beauty of the trees. The leaves had changed to brilliant shades of orange, yellow, red, and brown.

Sometimes it can feel as though we are stuck in one season—one that's challenging, exhausting, and overwhelming. We long for things to change for our child: for healing, for progress, for some kind of breakthrough. But what I realized while looking at those trees is that sometimes the change isn't seen in our child's situation; rather, it shows up in *us.*

We, too, go through seasons—seasons of growth, learning, and inner transformation. Although we may not see the transformation we hope for in our child, God is doing something in *us.* He is shaping our hearts, strengthening our faith, and giving us new perspectives. Just as the trees transition from one stage to the next, we are also being renewed with each passing season.

God is working in your heart. So if you find yourself in a season that feels hard and unchanging, remember that even if the situation stays the same, you are growing.

AFFIRMATION:

I embrace the seasons of my life, trusting that God is transforming me even when my circumstances remain the same.

28

Whether you turn to the right or to the left, your ears will hear a voice behind you, saying, "This is the way; walk in it."

—*Isaiah 30:21*

I learned to ride a bike when I was seven, full of curiosity and maybe just a little bit of fear. My sister was riding in the backyard and I asked her to teach me. With no training wheels, no big plan, just her voice steady in my ear, she placed me on the bike and told me to pedal. "I'm going to let go," she warned, "but you just keep pedaling." And I did. I shouted, "I've got it! I've got it!" and I was off. I didn't know how to stop yet, but that didn't matter: I was riding.

I think about that moment often, especially now as a parent raising a child with special needs. There are days when we don't have all the answers. Like when we ride that bike for the first time, we're wobbly, we're a little scared, and we're going fast. We may want instructions, guarantees, and maybe a few more hands to hold us up, but God's voice in our ear gently says, *Just keep pedaling. I'm right here.*

We may not know what tomorrow brings, but we're

moving forward inch by inch. And God promises to guide us, even when we fall.

So, today, take comfort that the journey doesn't require perfection—just a willing heart to keep pedaling.

AFFIRMATION:

Today, I keep pedaling, focusing not on perfection but on moving forward inch by inch.

29

[God] has made everything beautiful in its time. He has also set eternity in the human heart; yet no one can fathom what God has done from beginning to end.

—*Ecclesiastes 3:11*

Maison was diagnosed with severe autism when he was two years old. He was labeled nonverbal. When I first got that news, I didn't know how to take it. I stared at the paper and thought, *Severe? What will that mean for him?* My heart immediately began to ache, but there was never a moment when I didn't talk to God about Maison and his diagnosis. I never stopped talking to Him about my son's voice even when the doctors said he might never speak. I never stopped seeking His plan for Maison's future, his joy, and his place in the world.

Waiting for a breakthrough can be one of the hardest tests of faith. We yearn for progress and answers for what seems like an eternity. Ecclesiastes 3:11 reminds us that although we might perceive a delay, God's plan is good.

I am reminded of a story about Jason Arday, a young autistic man from London.* He is almost forty years old

* "Jason Arday Appointed Professor of Sociology of Education at University of Cambridge," Cambridge News, February 23, 2023, https://news.educ.cam.ac.uk/230223-jason-arday.

today, but he didn't speak at all until he was eleven. He didn't learn to read or write until he was eighteen. And now Jason is the youngest professor at the University of Cambridge. As his parents were raising him, they were likely unsure of what was ahead.

God's plan is greater than any plan we can ever have for our child, even when that plan looks *different* from what we'd hoped. Some children may never do what the world calls remarkable, but their very existence is a miracle. Their lives carry deep purpose, and their worth is woven into every breath they take. God's love for them—and His plan for them—is full of wonder, even in quiet places. Always remember that.

AFFIRMATION:

God's plan for me and my child is good.

30

> The Spirit of God has made me;
> the breath of the Almighty gives me life.
> —*Job 33:4*

Close your eyes and take a deep breath. Can you feel the air going in and out of your nostrils? The air you breathe is invisible, but you know it's there. It sustains you, fills your lungs, and gives you life. Just as you trust the air to give you oxygen, know that God is here with you. He is as present and vital as the very breath you take—always near, always caring.

Remember this: The same God who created the heavens and earth, the One who breathed life into Adam, is the One who breathes life into you each day. His Spirit is within you, renewing you, giving you strength every moment.

God is not just a distant observer; He is your constant source of life and strength. The Spirit of God has made you, and the breath of the Almighty gives you life. He has equipped you for this journey and will never leave your side. As you care for your child, remember to also care for yourself by drawing near to the source of life. In God's presence, you will find the rest, energy, and strength you need.

Let each breath be a reminder of His life-giving presence in your life.

AFFIRMATION:

Today, I breathe in God's love and exhale my worries.

31

Love your neighbor as yourself.
—*Matthew 22:39*

A famous saying tells us not to pour from an empty cup, but sometimes we find ourselves running on fumes, drained and exhausted and uncomfortable with the thought of prioritizing our own needs.

Why is it that we're often so comfortable running on empty? For some, it's because we feel guilty for taking time for ourselves, worried we're being selfish for needing a break. For others, running on empty is familiar, and the familiar way feels easier than changing for a better way. But how can we love and care for others if we don't take the time to care for ourselves?

Filling our cup doesn't equate to neglecting our responsibilities or the needs of our children; it simply means we're replenishing the well from which we draw. When we take moments to rest, recharge, and focus on our own well-being, we are better equipped to love, serve, and care for those around us. It's not selfish; it's necessary.

Be intentional about filling your cup today. It doesn't have to look perfect or take much time. Find a quiet minute, do some self-care, ask for help, take a fifteen-minute nap, or spend a few moments doing something you love to do.

When we prioritize our own needs, we are honoring the way God designed us to live: a balanced life where we can pour out to others without becoming empty ourselves.

AFFIRMATION:

I will take time to fill my cup, knowing that by caring for myself, I can better care for my child and those around me.

32

> Whoever believes in me, as the Scripture has said, "Out of his heart will flow rivers of living water."
>
> —*John 7:38*, ESV

Some days feel like you're walking through a desert. The days are long, the challenges overwhelming, and we find ourselves thirsting for strength and encouragement. Jesus offers us a promise: a river of living water that brings life and hope to our weary hearts.

This living water is more than just refreshment; it's the life-giving presence of Jesus within us. When we believe in Him, He fills us with His Spirit, renewing us from the inside out. It's like finding a cool stream in the middle of the desert—a place where we can rest, drink deeply, and find the strength to keep going.

The living water Jesus gives sustains us in often quiet, unseen ways. It doesn't always look like instant relief or a sudden burst of joy. Sometimes it's the peace that steadies us through a meltdown, the patience that shows up in the middle of chaos, or the gentle whisper reminding us that we're not alone. It's the strength to take one more step, breathe through the overwhelm, and show up again tomorrow. It's His presence that carries us—not by removing the hardship but by entering into it with us and offering rest in the middle of it all.

So, by "drink deeply," I mean pausing and taking note of the strength sustaining you. You can lean into that strength by whispering a quick prayer, turning on a worship song, recalling a verse, or just saying "Jesus, help me." These small moments become the streams where His living water flows, refreshing our spirit and keeping us rooted in love even on the hardest days.

Jesus is with us. He understands our struggles and is faithful to renew our strength, giving us what we need to continue loving and caring for our children.

Today, let's take a moment to drink deeply from the river of living water that Jesus offers. Let His love and strength flow into our hearts, bringing life, hope, and the ability to keep moving forward, one step at a time.

AFFIRMATION:

Jesus, the Living Water, sustains me, refreshes me, and strengthens me so I can face the challenges of today. With His help, I continue this journey with love and hope.

33

> The wisdom that comes from heaven is first of all pure; then peace-loving, considerate, submissive, full of mercy and good fruit, impartial and sincere.
>
> —*James 3:17*

As a parent raising a child with congenital heart disease, I've learned how crucial it is to protect my own heart physically and emotionally.

Many of us have experienced hurtful comments, often from those closest to us: family members who criticize our parenting or make insensitive remarks about our children. It's incredibly painful, and it's natural to feel hurt or even be brought to the verge of tears. I've been there myself, and it led me to make a tough but necessary decision: to set healthy boundaries.

Boundaries aren't about being mean or shutting people out; they're about preserving our emotional and spiritual well-being so that we can continue to love and care for our children. By guarding our hearts, we create a space where peace can flourish, allowing us to be the parents our children need without being drained by negativity.

Setting these boundaries is an act of self-compassion and a way to protect our family's peace. It's a way of ensuring that we have the strength and clarity to meet the unique challenges we face every day. When you find that someone in your life continues to bring you or your child down, spend a few moments in prayer. Ask God for wisdom and clarity on how to set healthy boundaries with grace. He promises to give wisdom generously to those who ask (see James 1:5). Boundaries guided by prayer are made not from fear or frustration but from a desire to protect what God has entrusted to us: our hearts, our children, and our peace.

Let God lead your heart as you discern where to draw the line with people's judgment and comments and how to walk in both truth and love. When we set boundaries prayerfully, we honor God and make room for His peace to dwell in our homes.

AFFIRMATION:

I guard my heart with wisdom, grace, and love, setting boundaries that protect my well-being and my family's peace.

34

> Those who hope in the LORD
> will renew their strength.
> They will soar on wings like eagles;
> they will run and not grow weary,
> they will walk and not be faint.
> —*Isaiah 40:31*

There's a saying that doing the same thing repeatedly and expecting different results is a form of insanity. We can often feel like we need to be everything to everyone, but when this consistently outweighs the simple act of caring for ourselves, it becomes a kind of self-sabotage. As a mother, I find myself pouring my energy into caring for my children, only to realize later that I've neglected my own well-being. I'm usually exhausted by the time I think of myself. But this shouldn't be the norm. I've learned the hard way that it's crucial to take moments to recharge.

To counter this cycle, I've made it a goal to find at least one moment of joy at least every month. These moments are often simple: sitting by the lake and soaking in the scenery, getting a mani-pedi, curling up with my favorite fuzzy blanket and a good show, or diving into a great book. Whatever brings me joy—even for just a moment—I intentionally lean into it.

Recently, my husband gently reminded me how much sunshine lifts my spirits. So, I went out and let myself enjoy the day—and it truly brought me joy. These small steps to care for myself help me stay balanced, refreshed, and ready for whatever comes next.

By taking care of ourselves, we not only benefit but also become better equipped to support our children. Let's remember that in seeking these moments of renewal, we are honoring the promise that God will give us the strength to soar and keep moving forward.

AFFIRMATION:

By honoring my need for self-care and finding my moments of joy, I receive God's promise of renewal.

35

> Let us not become weary in doing good, for at the proper time we will reap a harvest if we do not give up.
>
> —*Galatians 6:9*

Living in Texas means when it's hot, it's really hot. As I went for a walk recently, I started to feel winded in the heat and thought about turning back. But then I tried some self-talk: "Keep going, Camille. Keep going." Despite the discomfort, I knew my body needed to move, soak in some sunshine, and push through.

Endurance is the ability to weather unpleasant or difficult processes without giving way. As parents raising children with special needs, we embody endurance every day. The challenges we face can be overwhelming, and it's easy to feel like giving up when the road gets tough. But just like with that walk in the heat, we know deep down that pushing through is necessary for our own growth and well-being and for the well-being of our child.

In those moments when we feel winded and tired of life itself, when we want to turn back and retreat, let's remember that God is with us, gently guiding us forward. Even when the steps feel small or slow, each one still moves us further along. Keep pushing through—not so much in a white-knuckle, desperate sort of way but in a patient, steady, compassionate one. You've got this.

AFFIRMATION:

With God's presence and strength, I walk this journey with gracious endurance.

36

> The Spirit helps us in our weakness. We do not know what we ought to pray for, but the Spirit himself intercedes for us through wordless groans.
>
> —*Romans 8:26*

Prayer is not a mere ritual; it is a lifeline for weary hearts and minds. It's a sacred conversation with God where we pour out our fears, frustrations, and hopes, trusting that He hears us and cares deeply about our struggles. For us parents of children with special needs, prayer allows us to release the many burdens we carry into the hands of the One who is infinitely capable.

There are moments when words fail us—when the weight of the day feels overwhelming. Even in those moments, prayer remains powerful. Romans 8:26 reminds us that the Spirit intercedes for us when we do not know what to pray for. A simple sigh or tear reaches the heart of God as surely as any eloquent word.

Prayer shifts our focus from what we cannot control to the One who holds all things in His hands. It doesn't always change our circumstances immediately, but it transforms us, giving us the resilience and peace we need to face each day. There were nights when my son's meltdowns felt relentless and I didn't know how I would make it to morning. In those moments, I whispered prayers—sometimes through tears—and felt God's presence wrapping me in comfort. Prayer didn't take away the difficulty, but it gave me the courage to keep going.

I encourage you to make prayer a regular part of your life—not just in moments of crisis but in everyday moments as well. Speak to God as you would a trusted friend. Share your victories, your fears, and your desires. He is listening and He delights in every conversation with you.

AFFIRMATION:

I trust in God's ability to hear and respond to my heart's cry.

37

We know that in all things God works for the good of those who love him, who have been called according to his purpose.

—*Romans 8:28*

I was a trained chef, and the kitchen was my canvas. I knew how to build flavor, layer texture, and create something beautiful out of seemingly random ingredients. Nothing was wasted—not the bitter, the bland, or the bold. Each one had a purpose in the final dish.

When my son was diagnosed with autism, I stepped out of the kitchen and into a different kind of calling. The world I once knew—measured and plated just right—became unpredictable. I didn't leave my culinary degree behind; I just began to understand it in a new light.

God started speaking to me through what I already knew: He's the Master Chef, and this life we're living—even in all its broken pieces—is still a dish in progress. Some days are sweet. Some are salty. Some taste bitter going down. But He doesn't throw any of it away. He's using it all.

Caregiving, like cooking, takes time. Patience. But the finished product? It's worth every effort. Because God isn't just feeding others through our story; He's feeding *us* too.

So if you feel as though your life looks nothing like you expected, if you wonder what God is doing with the hard, messy, or mundane parts of your journey, remember that He's using every ingredient. You haven't missed your purpose; you're living it right now.

AFFIRMATION:

God is using every ingredient of my story to create something beautiful. Nothing is wasted in His hands.

38

> The Lord is my shepherd, I lack nothing.
>
> He makes me lie down in green pastures,
>
> he leads me beside quiet waters,
>
> he refreshes my soul.
>
> —*Psalm 23:1–3*

The constant demands of caregiving can make it seem like there's no time for rest, no space to breathe, and no moment to renew our weary hearts. Yet God, our shepherd, lovingly invites us to find peace in His presence.

Even when the world around us is loud, God knows how to guide us to moments of calm. When we feel depleted and unsure, He offers the comfort of His care, and in Him we lack nothing. For every need we have—physically, emotionally, and spiritually—He provides, moment by moment.

So many times, I have felt I was running on empty after long days and nights when I could barely hold it together mentally after being in the hospital for days with Maison. Yet in the early morning as I sip my coffee in the silence before my family wakes up, I feel God's nearness. When I pause to breathe and whisper a simple prayer like "Lord, I need You," I sense His peace. Sometimes He shows up through a worship song playing in the background, a verse that pops into my mind, or a text from a friend reminding me that I'm not alone.

He shepherds me by giving me what I didn't even know I needed: the strength to try again, the grace to let something go, or the comfort of His steady presence when no one else understands. I've learned that receiving His care doesn't always mean escaping the hard parts of the day; it means knowing I can walk through them with God right beside me.

Take a moment today to seek His presence and allow Him to restore your strength and renew your spirit. Trust in His love, knowing that in His care, you are never without what you need.

AFFIRMATION:

I choose to find peace in God's presence, knowing He provides all I need for each day.

39

> God is our refuge and strength,
> an ever-present help in trouble.
> —*Psalm 46:1*

Yesterday, I started my day in prayer and spent some time reading the Bible. I felt a strong pull to read scriptures about Jesus as our helper, and I was deeply encouraged by the reminder that He desires to help us in every area of our lives, not just in the desperate 911 situations.

Later that morning, I took Maison to church. We had been there for only about five minutes when Maison had a full-blown meltdown. I did my best to comfort him, but it quickly became clear that staying would be too overwhelming for him, so I decided we should leave. But you know, nothing about leaving saddened me. In fact, I felt an overwhelming sense of peace and gratitude. That morning, I had taken time to fill my cup and connect with God, so even though I left church early, I didn't feel like I was missing anything. As I sat in the car with Maison, I thought about the morning's verse again and was reminded that Jesus helps us not only in the big moments but also in the everyday disappointments, the quiet sacrifices, and the unexpected changes of plans.

Jesus helped Peter when he was gripped by fear and

sinking in the Sea of Galilee (see Matthew 14:30–31). He helped the woman with the issue of blood, stopping in a crowded street to heal her and speak to her heart (see Mark 5:25–34). He helped the widow at Nain (see Luke 7:11–15), meeting her in her grief and restoring what she had lost. In every situation, Jesus noticed, He moved toward, and He provided.

Jesus still does the same for us today. He sees us in the overwhelm, in the parking lot after leaving church, and in the tears we try to hold back. And He helps. In every moment, He helps.

AFFIRMATION:

My God helps me. He walks with me and guides me through every part of this journey.

40

> Come with me by yourselves to a quiet place and get some rest.
>
> —*Mark 6:31*

One Sunday, my oldest son and I went to church, just the two of us. On the way home, I suggested, "Let's grab something to eat." His eyes lit up. "Yes! This can be like our mental health day away from Maison." I was taken aback—not because he said it but because he *needed* to. In that moment, I realized my eighteen-year-old still needed me, still craved time to be seen apart from his role as the big brother. He needed permission to acknowledge the emotional weight he carried and to put it down without guilt. I told him I was proud of him for being honest, and I promised to be more intentional about giving him that space.

Loving all our family well means noticing the quiet ones, the strong ones, the ones who never complain but still carry so much. It means creating moments for them to be fully themselves—heard, seen, and poured into. Jesus knew we'd need rest, and He offered it not just for the weary but also for the overlooked. When we care for the whole family, we're creating a more supportive and balanced environment for our child with special needs too.

In today's verse, Jesus said to His disciples, "Come with me by yourselves to a quiet place and get some rest." Even the Son of God acknowledged the need for rest and personal care. Just as He recognized the importance of taking time to rejuvenate, we, too, must remember to care for ourselves and our other loved ones besides just our special-needs child.

Simple acts of love and understanding go a long way. Time for family activities, opportunities to listen to each person's concerns, and celebrations for every family member's achievements all help the entire family unite and thrive.

AFFIRMATION:

I cherish every member of my family. We are united in love and strength, and together we grow in grace and joy.

41

> He is my rock and my salvation;
> he is my fortress, I will not be shaken.
> —*Psalm 62:6*

God is our unshakable rock. When the future seems uncertain and our spirits feel weary, we can find comfort in knowing that our Lord is our reliable source of support through every challenge.

But what does it really mean that God is our rock? For me, it means He is my calm when life feels chaotic.

God as my rock means I don't have to hold everything together, because He already is. It means I can return to Him again and again and find steadiness in the middle of my storm. That's where I draw my peace and clarity. That's how I take my next breath when I feel like I can't.

Nothing may seem sure right now. You may not be able to count on a good night's sleep tonight, a pleasant doctor's visit, or the next milestone. Even when all the ground beneath us is shifting, Jesus is our unmovable rock. We can count on Him to be our help today, tomorrow, and always. His steadfast presence offers us reassurance and peace. Trust that He will guide us through each day, fortifying us with His strength and enveloping us in His love.

Take a moment to think about the areas of your life that feel shaky right now. Where are you feeling unsure, stretched thin, or overwhelmed? Bring those things to God in prayer. Ask Him to be your anchor in those specific places. Then reflect on where you've seen His steadiness—maybe in the comfort of a daily routine, a faithful friend, or even the strength you didn't know you had until you needed it.

Lean on Him, draw strength from His promises, and let His unwavering support lift you through the trials. He is your constant when life is anything but.

AFFIRMATION:

The Lord is my rock.
I trust in His unshakable presence.

42

Even though I walk
    through the darkest valley,
I will fear no evil,
    for you are with me;
your rod and your staff,
    they comfort me.
—*Psalm 23:4*

We often find ourselves standing in the gap between the world and our special-needs kids. We are having to fight for services, ensure that our children are seen and understood, and advocate for their needs. Remember, you are not alone in the gap. Just as you advocate for your child, Jesus advocates for you as His beloved child. He stands beside you, interceding on your behalf and carrying your burdens when they become too heavy.

When the fight seems endless, take comfort in knowing that the same power that raised Jesus from the dead is at work within you, giving you strength, courage, and wisdom.

Advocating for your child is a divine calling, one that mirrors Jesus's own love and care for you. Every time you speak up, push forward, and refuse to give up, you are reflecting His heart—a heart that never stops advocating, loving, and believing in you. Trust that He sees your efforts, knows your struggles, and will equip you with everything you need to continue the journey.

AFFIRMATION:

As I advocate for my child, I trust that Jesus is advocating for me.

43

> May the God of peace . . . equip you with everything good for doing his will, and may he work in us what is pleasing to him, through Jesus Christ, to whom be glory for ever and ever. Amen.
>
> —*Hebrews 13:20–21*

As parents, we often start out with a vision of fostering independence and growth. We don't want to be overbearing or stifle our child's potential, yet when a diagnosis alters the course of our journey, we may find ourselves thrust into a role we never anticipated—one that requires us to be extra vigilant, fiercely protective, and more involved than we ever thought possible.

Initially, this shift can be disorienting. We might feel guilty about suddenly needing to become a hovering parent, focusing more time on our child with special needs than on the rest of our children, not because we want to but because we have to. We worry that becoming more involved means crossing into overprotection. However, in embracing this role, we are not abandoning our ideals; we are adapting to the unique needs of our child. This newfound vigilance is not about control but about love—ensuring that our child receives the care and support they need to thrive.

God knew our journey would require us to evolve. He has equipped us with the empathic heart, watchful eyes, resilient energy, and enduring patience needed to fulfill our role. We are not hovering parents. We are learning to be present in the ways that best support our child's needs. Embrace this role with confidence, and trust that He is guiding you with purpose and care.

AFFIRMATION:
I am present, attentive, and exactly the support my child needs.

44

The LORD will watch over your coming and going
both now and forevermore.

—*Psalm 121:8*

I took Maison to a park the other day. It wasn't fenced in, which meant I had to keep a close eye on him because he might suddenly run off and put himself in danger. I followed him around, pushing him on the swing, going down the slide with him, and running alongside him. Every move he made, I was right there, watching carefully.

Nearby, I saw another mom sitting on a bench with a book while her kids played. I thought, *Our experiences are so different.* She could relax and enjoy her time at the park, while I had to stay constantly alert.

But in that moment, I realized our role as parents isn't defined by how easy things are; it's defined by the love and care we put into every day. The challenges of caregiving parents may be different, but they bring out a special kind of love and strength in us. It might seem like our journey is harder or less carefree compared to that of others, but we are showing an unwavering commitment to our children. Even though our path requires more vigilance, it is also filled with immense grace and deep purpose.

Let's remember that our love for our children is a reflection of God's love for us. We are not alone on this journey. We are supported and strengthened by Him each day.

AFFIRMATION:

My vigilance shows God's love, and I am never alone on this journey.

45

> Each one should test their own actions. Then they can take pride in themselves alone, without comparing themselves to someone else.
>
> —*Galatians 6:4*

There are moments when we sit with friends or family members, listening to them share stories of their children's milestones: first words, school achievements, weekend sports wins. And while we smile, part of us aches. It's not jealousy; it's grief. Our child's journey just looks different. And sometimes that difference feels invisible in a room where everyone else seems to be moving at the same pace as one another.

It's in those lonely moments that comparison creeps in. But here's the truth: Your child's growth matters just as much as other children's. Their milestones are not "less than"; they're just not the kind that people are used to talking about. So, what do we do in those conversations?

We start sharing. "He used his communication device to ask for juice this week. We've been working on that for months." Or "She made it through the grocery store without getting overwhelmed. That was huge for us." These moments are victories, they're hard-won, and they deserve to be celebrated out loud.

You don't have to stay silent when the conversation turns. Your child is worth bragging about too. And every time you speak their story, you make room for someone else who might feel as though their child's journey doesn't fit the mold either.

AFFIRMATION:

I will not be consumed by sorrow or comparison.
I celebrate my child's unique journey and
trust God's plan for their life.

46

> Do not conform to the pattern of this world, but be transformed by the renewing of your mind.
>
> —*Romans 12:2*

I used to think I had to put everything and everyone else first. There was always something urgent: a therapy appointment to schedule, a behavior plan to review, an insurance claim to fight, a school meeting to prepare for. Then there were the moments no one saw: washing soiled sheets in the middle of the night, calming sensory overload meltdowns, holding back tears while advocating for basic understanding. I kept telling myself I'd rest later, process later, breathe later.

But later never came. One day, I found myself feeling frozen in my car in the driveway—engine off, hands gripping the steering wheel like it was the only thing holding me together. And then I broke. I sobbed—loud, aching sobs that came from a place so deep that I didn't even know I was carrying that much pain. I couldn't move. I couldn't pretend anymore. The weight of it all had finally caught up with me.

That moment changed everything. I realized that maintaining mental health is not a luxury; it's a necessity. I couldn't keep pouring from an empty cup. Instead, I needed to check in with myself—to cry, to journal, to breathe, to talk to someone, to do whatever helped me feel human again. Taking care of my mental health wasn't a selfish act; it was an act of survival. It was how I would keep showing up—not just surviving the days but also living them with presence and love.

Whether it's through therapy, community, or moments of rest, take care of yourself. Make time to breathe, pray, and seek support when needed. You are not alone in this; God's peace, which surpasses all understanding (see Philippians 4:7), is guarding your heart and mind.

AFFIRMATION:

I am worthy of care and rest and will seek out what I need to be healthy and whole for myself and my loved ones.

47

Let everything that has breath praise the LORD!
—*Psalm 150:6,* ESV

What a relief to realize that joy isn't some treasure hidden away in an idyllic, trouble-free life. Joy is present here, with us right now, woven into the fabric of our everyday. The difference between a stressful day and a joyful day often comes down to what we pay attention to. Let's not pretend we can ignore the challenges and the difficulties, but we can make an intention to also see the little wins and the beauty of our everyday lives.

Don't overlook the small glimmers. It is usually in these little things where we find the most profound happiness and connection. A shared smile, a giggle, a gentle touch—these moments are worthy of celebration. Embrace them fully.

Today, direct your attention to the little joys in your life. Maybe it's the warmth of a spontaneous hug, a golden sunray slanting through the window, or the way your child's eyes light up when they see a favorite toy. Let the joy carry you through the day.

AFFIRMATION:

I celebrate the joy and beauty all around me.

48

> The LORD is my strength and my shield;
> my heart trusts in him, and he helps me.
> —*Psalm 28:7*

The first time Maison was admitted to the pediatric intensive care unit, I sat by his bedside in a hard chair. Machines beeped and doctors and nurses moved in and out while I sat frozen, unsure what I was supposed to do except be there.

I didn't question if God saw what was happening; I knew He did. I didn't doubt His presence, but I needed reassurance that He really did have our lives in His hands. I had to ask, *Is this really part of the story You wrote for my baby? For me?*

I felt a quiet presence—not loud or dramatic but steady. God didn't change the monitors beeping or the diagnosis, but He gave me peace and calm. When I could barely whisper a prayer, He held my heart. When I was too tired to be strong, He reminded me, *You don't have to be, because I am.*

Psalm 28:7 became a lifeline. It didn't promise that the storm would pass quickly, but it promised I wouldn't drown. God was my strength—not the kind that makes me immune to tears but the kind that helps me keep going even while they fall. He was my shield—not one that blocks every hard thing but one that keeps me from being crushed.

If you're walking through a moment that feels just as fragile and frightening as my experience, I want you to know you're not forgotten. God sees you. He hasn't turned away. He's not surprised. He knew this moment would come, and He's been preparing you, carrying you, and surrounding you all along.

AFFIRMATION:

God saw this moment before I ever walked into it. He is not surprised; He is not absent. He is my strength when I am weak and my shield when I am breaking.

49

> God shows his love for us in that while we were still sinners, Christ died for us.
>
> —*Romans 5:8*, ESV

As caregiving parents, we carry so much weight. We advocate, manage appointments, monitor progress, and strive to be present, all while juggling everyday life. We do an incredible amount of work with great attention and care. And still, there are moments we feel like we're falling short. Maybe it's the day we lost our patience. Or the time we missed a signal that our child was overwhelmed. Or the quiet guilt we carry when we wonder if we're doing enough.

But even in those moments, God's love doesn't shift. He doesn't keep a scorecard. He's not tallying our failures or withholding affection until we "get it right." Today's verse reminds us that His love met us at our lowest—not our best—and *still chose us.* That's the kind of love we reflect when we care for our special-needs children. It's not based on performance, milestones, or how put-together things look. It's rooted in commitment. In presence. In grace.

Maybe today you need to be reminded that you are not alone in your imperfect parenting. God is cheering you on, not critiquing from afar. His love is constant, and it covers every moment: the ones you're proud of and the ones you wish you could do over.

You can breathe knowing you are loved no matter what.

AFFIRMATION:

Even in my stumbles, I am not disqualified.
God's love for me is constant and unconditional.

50

> If our hearts condemn us, we know that God is greater than our hearts, and he knows everything.
>
> —*1 John 3:20*

For parents of children with special needs, guilt often becomes a constant companion. We question whether we're doing enough, wonder if we could have done something differently, and feel the weight of decisions we had no control over. It's a heavy burden to carry, and too often it robs us of the joy and peace we deserve. But I want to remind you—and myself—that guilt does not define us as parents.

We do the best we can with the knowledge, resources, and love we have in every moment. There's no perfect path, no magical formula that could have changed our child's journey. It's easy to look back and think, *What if?* But grace invites us to look forward, embracing the beauty of what we're building with our child now.

Carrying guilt doesn't make us better parents; it only makes the road harder. What our child needs most is our love, not our perfection. They need us present, not weighed down by mistakes we can't undo. Each day is a new opportunity to extend grace to ourselves, just as we do for them.

AFFIRMATION:

I release the guilt I carry and embrace grace.
I am doing my best, and that is enough.

51

> I will extol the Lord at all times;
> his praise will always be on my lips.
> —*Psalm 34:1*

There's something powerful about the sound of our voices lifted in prayer and worship, especially as parents raising children with special needs. Life can be chaotic, but I believe there is power in raising our voices, even when words seem hard to find.

Prayer and worship are more than rituals; they are lifelines. They give us space to release what we can't carry alone and remind us that we are held in something greater than our fears. When we open our mouths and let out even the smallest whisper of faith, we are pushing back against the stress, the exhaustion, and the uncertainty.

Sometimes that means the quiet moments of whispered prayers before our children go to bed. Other times it's the loud, tear-filled cries to God when we just don't know what else to do. And then there are the moments of worship when, despite everything, we declare that hope, joy, and peace are still ours to claim.

There's power in releasing a sound, whether it's a song of praise or a simple prayer of "Help me." Use your mouth as an instrument. Speak life into your situation. Sing peace over your home. Declare healing and strength over your child. Your voice has power.

Worship and pray aloud today and feel the power in your voice as you claim peace, strength, and hope for your family.

AFFIRMATION:

My voice is powerful. I will speak life, declare hope, and worship aloud, knowing my words carry strength and healing.

52

Cast all your anxiety on him because he cares for you.

—*1 Peter 5:7*

Everyone worries about the future at some level, but parents of children with special needs have a unique concern: *What will happen to my child when I am no longer here to care for them?* We know their every need, every comfort, every challenge, and every strength. The thought of leaving them without our care, without us as their constant support, can feel scary and overwhelming.

The world may not understand the depth of this fear, but God does. He knows the silent tears and the sleepless nights spent wondering and planning for a future in which we may not still be alive. Yet even in this fear, God calls us to cast our anxieties on Him, reminding us that He loves our children even more deeply than we do. His presence is not limited to our lifetime. His love and care for our children will continue long after we're gone. He is the ultimate protector, the One who watches over them day and night. We do our best to prepare and plan, but at the end of the day, we have to entrust our children to His care. He will provide the people, resources, and love they need to thrive, even when we can no longer be by their side.

But here's something you may not always recognize: The deep love and devotion you have for your child is evidence of God's heart toward them. The fact that He entrusted this child to *you*—a parent who would pray, plan, and fight for their future—is proof that He never intended for them to be without care. He chose you for a reason, and the same God who placed them in your arms will continue providing for them long after you're gone.

Take heart in knowing that the God who holds your heart also holds your child's future. His love knows no limits, and He will never leave them alone.

AFFIRMATION:

I entrust my child's future to God, knowing that His love and care will always surround them, even beyond my lifetime.

53

The eyes of the LORD range throughout the earth to strengthen those whose hearts are fully committed to him.

—*2 Chronicles 16:9*

There's an enduring strength that parents like my dear friend Tanisha possess—one that is forged in the fires of unimaginable challenges. Her son was born with kidney disease, later battled cancer and was healed, and lives with autism. He has spent more of his young life in hospitals than most of us can fathom. I've spoken to his mother in the midst of it all. Her strength is beyond words, the kind of strength that comes only from God.

As parents, we often find ourselves in roles we never expected. We become caregivers, advocates, and protectors. We have to navigate doctor's appointments, medical crises, and sleepless nights in the midst of trying to hold everything else together for our families. Tanisha is raising two other children, being a wife, and caring for her son—all while keeping faith alive. It is remarkable. And she'll be one of the first to tell us it's not easy.

Strength doesn't show up when things are easy; it shows up *because* things are hard. When the weight feels heaviest, when the tears won't stop, when you show up anyway—that's your strength at work. That's when Christ's power moves in you.

When we feel that we can't take another step, God meets us with supernatural strength. Strength that grows more active the harder things get. Strength that carries us through the tears, the exhaustion, and the uncertainty. We don't muster up this strength on our own; God pours His sustaining power into us.

So, for every parent walking this hard road, remember you are stronger than you know. Every difficult day is a day you've brought your strength to bear. And when you reach your limit, God is there to give you more.

AFFIRMATION:

I am strong, even when I feel weak.
God gives me supernatural strength to care for
my child and my family. In my exhaustion,
I find rest and renewal in Him.

54

> The LORD himself goes before you and will be with you; he will never leave you nor forsake you. Do not be afraid; do not be discouraged.
>
> —*Deuteronomy 31:8*

When we're navigating multiple diagnoses and unexpected changes, sometimes we can feel like we're caught in a relentless storm. We might find ourselves wondering how we'll manage everything or if we're even equipped for what's coming next. In these moments of chaos, Scripture's reassuring truth shines through: Everything's gonna be all right because God is with us.

This doesn't promise that everything will be perfect or that we will never experience challenges. Instead, it's a declaration of trust in God, who promises to lead us through it all. He doesn't guarantee a trouble-free journey, but He does promise that He will always strengthen us and walk beside us. It's about holding on to the assurance that He will guide and uphold us, no matter how daunting the path may seem.

Prayer is a powerful tool on this journey. It's not just about asking for what we need and want; it's also about claiming authority over fear and uncertainty. When we pray, we remind ourselves of God's promises and the strength He provides. Prayer is a declaration that despite the changes and challenges, we stand firm in His power and love.

So as you face each hurdle, remember that although things may not be perfect, you have the assurance that God's strength is your anchor. Trust that, even in the midst of the storm, everything's gonna be all right because you are held in His care. Take a moment to pray today. It doesn't have to be long or quiet or perfect. Whisper His name in the chaos, talk to Him while doing dishes, or breathe out a simple "Help me, Lord." Prayer doesn't need a special setting; it just needs your heart. He's listening, and He's near.

AFFIRMATION:

I trust in God's strength and authority.
I pray with confidence, knowing He is
with me in every challenge.

55

> A cheerful heart is good medicine,
> but a crushed spirit dries up the bones.
> —*Proverbs 17:22*

Laughter is a gift that brings both healing and hope.

One day, I had been up with Maison since four A.M., exhausted and trying to juggle a dozen things while feeling like I was failing at them all. Then, completely out of nowhere, he burst into the loudest giggle at something as simple as a crumpled straw. He has such a love for straws. His joy was so pure and contagious that I couldn't help but laugh with him, tears rolling down my cheeks—not from stress this time but from release. That moment changed the whole tone of my day. Laughter found me when I needed it most and reminded me to breathe.

Encourage yourself to embrace the humor around you. Seek out those moments of joy. Share a funny story, watch a comedy, ask a friend to send you a joke, or simply enjoy the laughter of your children. These moments aren't trivial; they are powerful. They lift our spirits, renew our strength, and remind us that happiness is a vital part of our journey.

When life gets heavy, it's easy to let stress take over. But laughter provides a much-needed break. It's a reminder that even during the toughest times, joy can still find its way in.

AFFIRMATION:
I will seek out laughter, knowing that joy strengthens and renews my spirit.

56

Man shall not live by bread alone,
but by every word that comes from the mouth of God.
—*Matthew 4:4*, ESV

Just as our bodies need food to keep going, our souls need nourishment too. And that nourishment comes from the Word of God.

It's easy to neglect our spiritual needs when life is hectic, but we have to remember that our souls require sustenance. When we take time to read God's Word and linger in His presence, we feed our hearts, minds, and spirits life-giving truth.

Just as we wouldn't go a whole day without eating, we shouldn't go long without the Word either. God's Word fills us, refreshes us, and equips us to handle whatever comes our way. It brings peace to chaos, hope to uncertainty, wisdom to confusion, and strength to weakness.

As you care for your family, remember to nourish your soul. Spending time in God's Word doesn't have to be quiet or uninterrupted for Him to speak to your heart. You could read a chapter on your phone while waiting in the car-pool line, play audio Scripture aloud in the kitchen, or write a verse on a sticky note and place it where you'll see it throughout the day. If you can't get a moment alone, read a Bible story with your kids. Even if it's just a few words you return to over and over throughout the week, let God's truth nourish you. He honors the minutes we set aside to listen and learn from Him, no matter how few those minutes may be.

AFFIRMATION:

Just as my body needs food, my spirit needs God's presence and the truth of His Word.

57

I will not leave you as orphans; I will come to you.

—*John 14:18*

Faith isn't always easy, especially when raising a child with a disability. There are days when we pray for a break-through, hoping for change, only to be met with silence, and we think, *God, where are You?*

We want to believe that things will get better, that He will move in the way we've prayed for. But when we don't see it, God can seem distant or, worse, as though He's not listening. In these moments, we're faced with the hard truth that faith isn't about what we see or hear; it does not rely on our circumstances. Faith is about trusting His goodness, even when our situation doesn't change. God's faithfulness isn't measured by what we see; it's measured by His unwavering presence with us in every twist and turn.

It reminds me of Naomi's story in the Bible. After losing everything, she returned home bitter and broken, believing that God had turned against her. But even in her sorrow, He was quietly at work through Ruth, redeeming Naomi's story in a way she couldn't have predicted. Just like Naomi, we might not recognize God's hand right away, but that doesn't mean He's absent. Sometimes

His greatest work is happening behind the scenes, even in the silence.

You may not see the changes you long for right now, but know this: He has not abandoned you. He comes to you. He walks with you in the hard days, in the unanswered prayers, in the "Why, God?" moments. Having faith means believing that He is working in ways we can't see—that when it's difficult to understand, He is still weaving beauty into our story.

AFFIRMATION:

My faith is rooted in God's unchanging goodness.
Even when I don't see the changes I long for,
I trust that He is with me, faithful and true.

58

He is the Rock, his works are perfect,
and all his ways are just.
A faithful God who does no wrong,
upright and just is he.
—*Deuteronomy 32:4*

God does not make mistakes. You've probably read that in the Bible or sung it in a worship song. Yet it can be a hard truth to reconcile when our children are given unfair difficulties.

But your child was knit together by the Creator of the universe—on purpose, with intention, and in love. Every detail, from the way they think to the battles they face, is seen and known by God. And though their body may carry pain or their mind may operate differently than most people's, they are not a mistake. They are deeply loved, eternally valuable, and crafted with purpose.

Yes, there is real grief we carry as parents, especially when watching our children suffer. Some children's bodies are broken by disease, some may not experience healing this side of heaven, and still, God's design and love remain. He holds their bodies, their stories, and their futures in His hands. His definition of *wholeness* isn't limited to what we can see; even in their limitations, even in pain, they are fearfully and wonderfully made.

So, let's hold space for both grief and gratitude. Heartache and holiness. Our child's body may be fragile, but their soul is radiant. And in God's eyes, they are whole. Our Father hasn't turned His face away; He is still working, still loving, and still present, right in the middle of it all.

AFFIRMATION:

My child is deeply loved by God, who makes no mistakes. My child's life is a reflection of His intentional love, and I trust His hand even when I don't understand His plan.

59

> Encourage one another and build each other up, just as in fact you are doing.
>
> —*1 Thessalonians 5:11*

Sometimes God sends help by way of a conversation, a late-night message from a fellow parent, or even a stranger's Instagram post that reads like your own thoughts. These moments may feel small, but they are not random; they are God's provision.

When my son was diagnosed with autism, I prayed for answers. I wanted direction, clarity, even miracles. What I received instead were people—voices of encouragement and shared wisdom and arms to help carry the load. One of the greatest gifts came in an unexpected way at the end of 2021, when I stumbled upon an audio app called Clubhouse. I felt led to start a space for moms like me, and I named it the Real Moms Club. It quickly grew into the largest parenting club on the app, and every Monday for a year, we (a group of moms and dads who logged in from all over the world) gathered virtually to laugh, cry, share, and strengthen one another.

That space became a lifeline—not just for me but also for many other parents raising children with special needs. It wasn't the doctors or teachers who got me through my hardest days; it was other parents who understood. They didn't hold back their wisdom or gatekeep their knowledge. Instead, they poured it out freely, making sure none of us felt alone. Looking back, I see clearly that it wasn't just community; it was divine connection.

God often meets our deepest needs through others. And while finding community doesn't always look the way we expect, He knows how to place the right people in our path: people who speak life when we feel like giving up and who remind us that we're not walking this road alone.

If you're still searching for that kind of support, don't give up. Ask God to guide your steps. Be open to unexpected connections. And remember, your story, your experience, your voice may be the answer to someone else's prayer too.

AFFIRMATION:

God places the right people in my life at the right time. I am open to His divine connections.

60

This is the day that the Lord has made;
let us rejoice and be glad in it.
—*Psalm 118:24*, ESV

Parents, you've made it to today. And let me remind you—*today* matters. Whether it's the start of your week or you're heading into the weekend, it's worth celebrating. You've been working hard, showing up for your child in ways that most people don't see. So, why not take a moment to celebrate your wins, big and small?

Now let's have some fun! Turn on your favorite song—something upbeat, something that makes you smile or brings back a happy memory. Get your child in on it if they're nearby. Whether you're in the kitchen, the living room, or even the car (safely parked, of course!), have a little dance party. Even if you've got two left feet or your child's rhythm is all their own, let the music carry you.

Feel that? That little boost of joy? Sometimes we get so focused on the day-to-day grind—doctor's appointments, therapies, homework, meltdowns—that we forget to celebrate all we've done and how far we've come. But joy is powerful. Even in the midst of challenges, we can laugh, move, and dance through the hard days.

So, let go of the worries for a moment. Let the music

lift your spirits and lighten your heart. You deserve it. And guess what? These small moments of fun can create some of the best memories for you and your child.

AFFIRMATION:

I am proud of the hard work I've done to care for and love my child well. I am a joyful, resilient parent, and I celebrate the good things.

61

> She is clothed with strength and dignity;
> she can laugh at the days to come.
> —*Proverbs 31:25*

Some strength is loud. It flexes to impress and strains to move mountains. And some strength is quiet—but just as powerful. It lives in the arms of a mother who trains her body so she can lift her twenty-six-year-old daughter every day. It lives in the mind of a woman who doesn't give up, even when the world around her doesn't know all she carries.

I have a friend who is one of the strongest people I know. Her daughter is blind, has a rare syndrome as well as autism, and has never been potty trained. She has to care for her as if she were a young toddler. My friend's life looks nothing like most, but when you meet her, you don't feel heaviness; you feel light. You feel joy. She experiences much difficulty, but she has chosen to be full of life anyway. She is so bright and absolutely beautiful.

She once told me, "I go to the gym not just for me but also so I can keep lifting my girl." That's the kind of love that moves heaven. That's the kind of faith that isn't loud and flashy—but it changes the atmosphere.

Maybe your life feels like hers: marked by effort that

most can't see. Maybe your days are filled with lifting, carrying, tending, and loving in ways no one else will ever fully grasp. I want you to know that God sees every ounce of strength you pour out. He honors every moment in which you choose love over bitterness. And He is renewing your strength day by day, even when you don't feel it.

You were chosen for this—not because you were the strongest but because you're willing to show up with grace, grit, and faith.

AFFIRMATION:

God sees the strength I give each day. He is renewing me with courage, love, and resilience.

62

> Those who look to him are radiant;
> their faces are never covered with shame.
> —*Psalm 34:5*

We know all too well the stares and judgment of others when our children behave in ways that aren't easily understood. Whether it's a public meltdown, quirky behavior, or something as simple as not meeting the arbitrary expectations of others, these moments can bring embarrassment and shame.

I once heard a story of a man who grew up with a disability. His father, rather than encouraging him, would react with disgust or anger whenever he made a mistake. This left deep wounds, making him feel small and ashamed of who he was. But as parents dedicated to helping our children thrive, we cannot give shame a place in our hearts or homes. Our children need to know they are loved and accepted just as they are, no matter their challenges or cognitive abilities. Our children's worth isn't determined by what society deems normal; it's defined by the love and purpose God has given them.

When the world tries to make you feel ashamed of your child's behavior, keep your head up. Don't be concerned with anyone else's perception. You are your child's greatest advocate and cheerleader. Encourage them, love them, and walk beside them proudly. God has entrusted them to you because He knows you're the one who can give them the strength and belonging they need to thrive. Every step, every triumph, every challenge is part of their journey—and yours.

AFFIRMATION:

I reject shame and judgment. My child is wonderfully made, and I support and encourage them with love and pride.

63

> He will cover you with his feathers,
> and under his wings you will find refuge;
> his faithfulness will be your shield and rampart.
>
> —*Psalm 91:4*

Have you ever felt like you were in a boxing ring, constantly defending and advocating? Some days it seems as though no one in the world is hearing you and you're left explaining your child's needs and your choices yet again.

Today, as I dropped Maison off at school, it was one of those moments. Already feeling worn down, I placed him in his special-needs stroller to help him get inside. As I walked in, the secretary looked us up and down and asked, "What's this?" She saw the stroller, but she didn't see the need behind it. Frustrated, I explained the situation again, and though she apologized, it left me thinking, *Why must we be in a constant state of correcting, advocating, and explaining?*

Moments like this sting. They bring a sense of weariness, a reminder that our journey doesn't match what the majority of those around us experience. It's okay to feel frustrated, but we can't let it consume us. When we feel defensive, God meets us there with perfect understanding. Jesus was misunderstood—by crowds, religious leaders, even His own family. People expected Him to be something He wasn't—to fix things in ways He never promised. So when we feel unseen or misjudged, we can take comfort in knowing that He truly understands. He's been there, and He stands with us now.

There will always be someone who doesn't get it, and there may be times when we feel judged or alienated. But we don't have to carry it all ourselves.

Let God be your strength, your peace, and your defender. He speaks through compassionate teachers, softens hearts in meetings, and sends helpers at just the right time. His defense isn't always loud and dramatic; it's often quiet and steady, wise and sure. He covers you with grace when others question your choices, and He affirms your heart when doubt creeps in. Take a deep breath and remember that He knows your heart, He knows your child, and He's got you both.

AFFIRMATION:

I release worry about others' judgment, and I rest in the truth that God, my defender, understands me and my child fully.

64

We walk by faith, not by sight.

—2 Corinthians 5:7, ESV

Today, I finally put up the Christmas tree, and what happened next caught me completely off guard. My sweet boy Maison started singing, "Santa Claus is coming to town." My husband and I looked at each other, wide-eyed, and said in unison, "He knows!" It was clear to us that at seven years old, Maison now understood the concept of Santa for the first time.

Moments like these take my breath away. As a parent of a child who does not communicate in typical ways, it is often hard to measure what they understand. But this moment reminded me of something powerful: Always presume competence.

Presuming competence means believing that our children understand far more than we see on the surface. It challenges us to let go of what we expect and to embrace what is. For us, this means learning to view the world through Maison's eyes instead of our own. It's not always easy; it stretches our faith and pushes us to trust in what we cannot see. But when we do, the rewards are breathtaking.

Our children are listening. They are learning. They are

taking in the world in ways we may never fully comprehend.

Celebrate those unexpected moments when their understanding shines through, and trust God with the rest. More things are happening than we realize. You may not always see progress, but it is happening. And when it shows up, it will bring you to tears in the best way possible.

AFFIRMATION:

I trust that my child is learning, growing, and thriving in more ways than I can see.

65

I praise you because I am fearfully and wonderfully made;
your works are wonderful,
I know that full well.

—*Psalm 139:14*

Birthdays are a big deal. The balloons, the cake, the friends gathered around singing—those are the moments we envision when we think of celebrating our children. But for many of us raising children with special needs, birthdays look quite different.

Maybe your child does not understand what a birthday is or what all the fuss is about; they do not like the loud singing or the sensory overload of a crowd. Or you send out invitations, but only a few people show up—or none. It's hard not to feel the sting of unmet expectations.

But here is the thing: A birthday is still a celebration of life, of your child's uniqueness, and of the incredible journey God has planned for them. Your child's value is not defined by how they celebrate or how many people join in; it is rooted in the fact that God made them wonderfully and fearfully.

If you find yourself in a quieter birthday moment, take a step back and look at your child. Their smile, their laughter, their calm contentment speak volumes. They may not understand a birthday the way we do, but they can feel your love. That love is what matters most.

Birthdays do not have to fit a mold. Whether it is a big party, a cozy family day, or just you whispering "Happy birthday" as they play, the celebration counts. God sees these moments and rejoices with you.

Your child's life is a gift. Every year is worth celebrating, no matter how it unfolds.

AFFIRMATION:

I celebrate my child's life with joy, knowing that each year is a precious gift from God.

66

> My flesh and my heart may fail,
> but God is the strength of my heart
> and my portion forever.
> —*Psalm 73:26*

After struggling to get Maison dressed one morning, I sat on the bathroom floor and cried. He was overwhelmed. I was frustrated. I had already raised my voice more often than I'd wanted to, and guilt crept in like an unwelcome guest. I kept thinking to myself, *You should've handled that better.* I replayed every moment, picking apart my tone, my response, my choices. But in the quiet that followed, I felt a gentle nudge from God: *You're not perfect. You're present. And that is enough.*

We put so much pressure on ourselves to be everything our children need. But God never asked us to be perfect. His grace meets us in the missteps, the second-guessing, and the messy middle of parenting. He doesn't measure our worth by how calm we stayed or how many therapies we scheduled. He sees the love behind our effort.

Parenting a child with unique needs takes courage and consistency, not perfection. And when we lean into God's strength instead of our own, we begin to understand the beauty of relying on Him. His grace doesn't run out when we fall short; it fills in the gaps where we can't.

AFFIRMATION:

Even in my weakness, God's grace is enough.
I release the pressure to be perfect, and I choose
to be present with love and trust.

67

Forget the former things;
do not dwell on the past.
See, I am doing a new thing!
Now it springs up; do you not perceive it?
—Isaiah 43:18–19

There's a quiet grief many of us carry: the letting go of the future we once imagined for our special-needs child. We dreamed of soccer games, school dances, best-friend sleepovers. We thought we knew how their life would unfold. And then came the diagnosis that changed everything.

It's not that we love our child any less. In fact, we love them more fiercely than ever. But some days, the grief of what we thought would be creeps in and we wonder if it's okay to mourn the dream while still embracing the beauty of what is.

The answer is yes.

God reminds us in Isaiah 43 not to cling to what once was—to open our hearts to the *new thing* He's doing. That doesn't erase the grief, but it gives hope. Our child may not follow the path we envisioned, but their journey is still holy. Still meaningful. Still filled with God's fingerprints.

He's writing a story in their life that's different, yes, but no less worthy. And He's inviting us to trust Him with the pen, even when we can't see the ending yet.

AFFIRMATION:
I release what I imagined and embrace the beauty of what is. God is doing a new thing in my child's life, and I trust Him with the journey ahead.

68

Learn to do right; seek justice.
Defend the oppressed.
Take up the cause of the fatherless;
plead the case of the widow.
—*Isaiah 1:17*

Few things feel more devastating than witnessing our child face rejection simply because of their disability. It's a pain that cuts deeply, leaving us feeling helpless and frustrated, wondering how anyone could fail to see the beauty and value in our child.

When stories like a group of students being denied access to a restaurant or a child being excluded from an activity come to light, it's hard not to feel crushed. For us advocates, when the world is unkind, the heartbreak can feel unbearable. God's heart aches along with ours. He sees our pain, hears our cries, and walks beside us as we fight for our child.

God equips us to be their voice and their champion, and He surrounds us with a community ready to stand alongside us in love and support. And in those moments of injustice when nothing we do makes a difference, we remember that discrimination does not get the final word. God does, and He speaks unfathomable love over our child.

AFFIRMATION:

God is close when the world feels far. I will not measure our joy by how others see us. My child is deeply loved, and I am doing holy work as their parent.

69

> A friend loves at all times,
> and a brother is born for a time of adversity.
> —*Proverbs 17:17*

Between therapy appointments, school meetings, and caregiving responsibilities, it's easy to let relationships take a back seat. Sometimes it can even feel as though the weight and messiness of your life might be too much for others to understand or bear.

Let me remind you that you are worthy of healthy, loving relationships—just as you are.

True relationships are built on understanding, empathy, and mutual support. The right people will see your child's diagnosis not as a burden but as a beautiful part of your story. They will celebrate your victories, stand beside you in the hard moments, and extend grace when life feels overwhelming.

It's okay to evaluate the relationships in your life. Not everyone is meant to walk this journey with you, and that's all right. But never let the fear of rejection and judgment stop you from seeking and nurturing meaningful connections. Whether it's a supportive spouse, a faithful friend, or a trusted mentor, God places people in our sphere to remind us that we are meant to do life together.

Spending time with others doesn't have to be elaborate or time-consuming. It can be as simple as a phone call while folding laundry, a quick voice note after a long day, or having a friend join you while you run. It's the presence, not the production, that fills the soul.

You are enough, and you are worthy of love, understanding, and connection.

AFFIRMATION:

God has created me for connection. I deserve to spend time with friends who uplift and encourage me.

70

> God created mankind in his own image,
> in the image of God he created them;
> male and female he created them.
>
> —*Genesis 1:27*

God gave every person unique marks: their fingerprints. There are more than eight billion people on earth, yet no two people share the same fingerprints. Even identical twins, with practically the same DNA, have distinct fingerprints. This is a beautiful reminder that God's creativity and design are beyond measure.

But in addition to admiring your child's uniqueness, have you noticed how they teach you to see the world differently? Maybe their way of communicating love is unconventional or the way they find joy in repetition has helped you slow down and appreciate moments you used to overlook. Perhaps their perseverance has shown you what true strength really looks like.

In these moments, big and small, we see a glimpse of God's image not just *in* our child but also *through* them. They become our unexpected teacher, drawing out parts of us we didn't know existed: deeper patience, fierce advocacy, and unconditional love. This journey of parenting a child with special needs isn't just about guiding them; it's also about being transformed ourselves to witness more of God in and around us.

AFFIRMATION:

My child was created in God's image, and through them I'm learning more about who God is: creative, patient, loving, and full of grace.

71

> To him who is able to do immeasurably more than all we ask or imagine, according to his power that is at work within us, to him be glory.
>
> —*Ephesians 3:20–21*

A diagnosis often comes with a list of "nevers":

"Your child will never walk."
"Your child will never speak."
"Your child will never live independently."

These words cut deep. They feel final, like the closing of a door before it's even been opened. But God calls us to a life of hope, not limitations. The "nevers" don't have to define our child. In fact, hope has a way of finding openings we never imagined. It's not just about proving others wrong; it's about seeing what God can do in our child and in ourselves.

There are countless stories of children who were told they would "never"—and yet they did. Why? Because someone believed in them. Someone chose to hope, push, encourage, and refuse to give up. Hope is contagious. When you hold on to hope for your child, you plant seeds of belief in them. They begin to see themselves not just in terms of their diagnosis but also as capable, loved, and purposed by God.

Hope keeps us moving forward. It keeps us praying, advocating, teaching, and believing. And when we trust in God, the author of our hope, we can be assured that He's writing a story greater than anything we could imagine.

So when you hear the word "never," let it ignite hope in your heart. Look at your child and take note of all the "yeses," "soons," and "maybes." Remember that with God, nothing is impossible.

AFFIRMATION:

I reject the "nevers" and choose, through Jesus, to hold on to hope for my child.

72

> Fix these words of mine in your hearts and minds; tie them as symbols on your hands and bind them on your foreheads. . . . Write them on the doorframes of your houses and on your gates.
>
> —*Deuteronomy 11:18, 20*

I've always had a special place in my heart for palm trees. There's something about them that immediately transports me to a warm, tropical paradise, even when I'm far from the coast. The way they stand tall and sway with the breeze fills me with a sense of calm. Recently, I brought a fake palm tree into my office space, a small yet meaningful attempt to create a joyful atmosphere around me. And you know what? Every time I glance at it, I can't help but smile.

Our surroundings play a significant role in shaping our mood and mindset. This is one of the reasons God urged the Jewish people to create physical reminders of His commands and promises. We can do the same. Maybe you love elephants, or perhaps you're drawn to mountains or something else entirely. Whatever brings you a sense of happiness, nostalgia, or awe, I encourage you to add it to your space. It doesn't have to be big or extravagant—just a small gesture to brighten your day and fill your heart with joy.

We must remember that joy isn't something we wait for; it's something we can cultivate in our own lives. We are in control of the environment around us. We can choose to fill our spaces with things that help us breathe deeply, smile, and remember the goodness of God's love for us.

AFFIRMATION:

Today, I will surround myself with reminders of God's goodness.

73

> Gracious words are a honeycomb,
> sweet to the soul and healing to the bones.
> —*Proverbs 16:24*

We're often our own worst critics, constantly second-guessing ourselves. *Did I handle that meltdown the right way? Did I miss something important at that appointment? Should I have been more patient?* But what if we spoke to ourselves with the same tenderness we offer our children? What if we traded *I should have . . .* for *I did the best I could today*? That simple shift can change everything.

God doesn't look at us with disappointment. He sees the heart behind our actions. He knows the exhaustion, the sacrifices, and the love that fuels every decision, even the ones we're unsure of. His grace covers the moments when we feel we've fallen short. It's not about perfection; it's about presence. And showing up faithfully, even on the hard days, matters more than we give ourselves credit for.

You are doing amazing work, and it's okay to speak kindly to yourself along the way. The same voice you use to reassure your child—*you* deserve to hear it too.

Giving yourself grace means choosing kindness over

criticism, patience over frustration, and understanding over guilt.

AFFIRMATION:
I am faithful with what God has entrusted to me.
I speak grace and life over myself.

74

Be devoted to one another in love. Honor one another above yourselves.

—*Romans 12:10*

Holidays can be a beautiful time of connection, laughter, and shared meals as well as, for many like us, an undercurrent of stress. Sometimes the questions and unsolicited advice from well-meaning relatives are more than we can handle.

Your child, with their unique needs and beautiful differences, deserves to be welcomed, not questioned. So do you. You show up every day as their advocate, their cheerleader, and their safe place, and that is no small thing. When the comments sting or the not-so-helpful hints pour in, take a deep breath and remember this: You are the expert on your child. God has equipped you to walk this path, not anyone else. Other people's opinions don't define your worth or your child's value. In fact, their words often come from a place of ignorance.

The holidays may not always feel like a sanctuary, but God can be your refuge. You can find strength in Him when the questions are too much. Perhaps this happens in a quiet moment of prayer in the midst of the chaos, when you ask for His peace to settle over you. Or maybe it's in recalling a scripture that speaks to your heart, like Psalm 46:1: "God is our refuge and strength, an ever-present help in trouble." It could be as simple as acknowledging His presence in the beauty of a winter sunset or the laughter of your child, reminding you that He is with you. When you feel overwhelmed, take a few deep breaths and consciously turn your thoughts to Him, visualizing His calming presence.

At the next family gathering, remember this: You are showing courage by showing up. You are building memories. You are teaching your child that they belong in every space. And if someone cannot meet you with love, support, and understanding, know that your heavenly Father already has.

AFFIRMATION:

I am my child's strongest advocate.

75

> Accept one another, then, just as Christ accepted you, in order to bring praise to God.
>
> —*Romans 15:7*

We know how deeply we want the world to embrace our children for who they are—not despite their differences but because of them. Yet before the world fully understands the beauty of our children, we have the sacred gift of showing them what it means to belong, starting in our own homes.

Belonging isn't about waiting for acceptance from the outside; it's about creating a space, day by day, where our children feel seen, safe, and celebrated. It's found in how we speak to them and about them, how we adapt the rhythms of our home to honor who they are, and how we show up—again and again—with love that doesn't waver. Home becomes their first glimpse of God's unconditional love—the place where they learn they don't have to change to be worthy of joy, belonging, or grace.

When others fail to see the beauty in our children's differences, it stings. But every time someone does see it—when a teacher goes the extra mile, when a friend shows kindness, when a stranger smiles with understanding—it's a glimpse of the way God values and celebrates our children. Acceptance is not just about fitting in; it's about belonging just as we are. When we model love and acceptance to our children, we are showing them that we know they are "fearfully and wonderfully made" (Psalm 139:14).

AFFIRMATION:

My child's differences are beautiful, valuable, and worthy of celebration, and my child will always belong in the space I've made for them.

76

> He gives strength to the weary
> and increases the power of the weak.
> —*Isaiah 40:29*

The words *relax* and *unwind* feel foreign to us parents of special-needs kids. While others can sip their coffee and let their children run carefree on the playground, we're scanning the environment, predicting meltdowns, and navigating stares. Survival mode isn't just a season; it's often our way of life.

But even in our perpetual state of being "on," God meets us in our weariness. Scripture reminds us that we are not walking this journey unassisted. He is our strength when our reserves are depleted and our shield when the weight of responsibility feels too heavy.

It's okay to acknowledge that this is hard. It's okay to admit that living on edge takes a toll. But it's also vital to remember that you're not shouldering this responsibility alone. God is with you, ready to help and renew your strength. Think back to a moment when your vigilance surprised even yourself—when your instincts kicked in just in time or when you made it through a night you thought would break you. That strength wasn't random;

that was God moving through you, covering you with His shield, and lifting you with His grace.

Lean into Him when it all feels like too much. Ask Him for the strength to make it through another day. And when those rare moments of rest appear—when your child is finally asleep or when help arrives—receive the rest without guilt.

AFFIRMATION:

God is my strength and my help, and
His grace sustains me in every moment.

77

> You will go out in joy
> and be led forth in peace;
> the mountains and hills
> will burst into song before you,
> and all the trees of the field
> will clap their hands.
>
> —*Isaiah 55:12*

God's joy isn't something we have to chase or earn; it's waiting for us in His creation, new experiences, and the smiles and laughter of our little ones as they take in the beauty. It's easy to feel stuck, overwhelmed, and uninspired, especially when it's as if life is on repeat. But refreshment is waiting at the simplest of places: outside the four walls in which we spend so much time.

When the heaviness sets in, give yourself the gift of a change of scenery, even just for a little while. Take your child outside, let the sun warm your face, and listen to the breeze rustling through the trees. Go to the zoo, walk in a park, visit the library, or explore a quiet trail. Nature and new surroundings have a way of gently reminding us of God's beauty and creativity, and they help reset our weary hearts.

When the weight of routines, appointments, and daily

struggles drains the joy right out of us, that's our cue to go marvel at the incredible world. Take heart: Stepping out doesn't mean you're shirking any responsibilities. It's an act of kindness to yourself, a way to renew your spirit, and an opportunity to anchor yourself in the truth that you and your child are part of a beautiful world.

AFFIRMATION:

Today, I will step outside, breathe deeply, and allow God's creation to renew my spirit.

78

> Jesus looked at them and said, "With man this is impossible, but with God all things are possible."
>
> —*Matthew 19:26*

When a parent receives a diagnosis for their special-needs child, a doctor often tries to give a clear picture of what it could mean for the child's life. They may tell us our child will never play sports, will never speak, or will need repeated surgeries. These are heavy words for any parent to hear. The future, once bright with limitless possibilities, can suddenly be filled with obstacles. The doctor's job is to outline the challenges, but that doesn't mean the story ends there.

I think of a young man, Nick Vujicic, who was born with no arms and no legs. His parents refused to limit him to only what others thought was possible. They chose hope and perseverance. He joined his high school wrestling team, grew up to marry and become a father, and today is a motivational speaker who inspires countless people. His parents didn't allow his diagnosis to define him; they held on to the possibility that he could have a fulfilling life despite what doctors said.

When we face these challenges, we can choose to stand firm in faith. He has a plan for our children—a plan for a future filled with meaning and joy. It might not look like what we imagined, but that doesn't mean it won't be beautiful. Regardless of any diagnosis, we keep our hope alive. We believe in good things to come for our children.

AFFIRMATION:

I believe that with God, all things are possible for my child. We will walk in hope, knowing that His power is at work in our lives.

79

She gave this name to the LORD who spoke to her: "You are the God who sees me," for she said, "I have now seen the One who sees me."

—*Genesis 16:13*

Much of our days are spent on work that no one sees, like cleaning medical equipment, arranging schedules, and changing diapers. And it feels as though no one truly knows all that we're navigating—not the long to-do lists, the sacrifices, the silent prayers, or the tears we cry in solitude. But God does.

He sees the sleepless nights, the unspoken fears, and the relentless hope you hold on to for your child's future. Every tear you've cried has been noticed and treasured by Him. Every sacrifice you've made is known to the One who understands the depth of your love.

God witnesses your entire life. His heart is moved by the way you care for your child. He is proud of you and delights in you.

Take a deep breath and let these words sink in: You are seen, you are valued, and you are loved. In the chaos of life, God holds you close, guiding you and strengthening you for each step of this path. You're doing an incredible job, even when it feels like no one notices.

AFFIRMATION:

I am seen by God, who knows all that I am and all that I do. I am doing enough, and I *am* enough.

80

> You make known to me the path of life;
> you will fill me with joy in your presence,
> with eternal pleasures at your right hand.
>
> —*Psalm 16:11*

Moments of joy can be very short. Yet something so brief can fill our souls with the strength and hope we need to keep going.

Moments of joy don't have to be big or extravagant. They're often found in the simplest experiences: a deep breath, a small treat, or a quiet pause. But their impact stays with us, anchoring us in gratitude and reminding us that God's goodness is present even in the chaos.

You don't need to wait for trickles of joy to find you; you can open opportunities for more joy to pour in. Here are a few ideas:

1. **Find a new hobby or revisit an old one.** Whether it's reading, gardening, painting, or learning a new skill, give yourself permission to enjoy something just for you, if only for ten minutes.
2. **Eat your favorite nostalgic snack.** Treat yourself to something that brings back happy memories from your childhood or simpler times. Let it spark comfort and joy.

3. **Get outside.** Step into nature for a walk, sit under a tree, or enjoy a quiet moment on the porch. Fresh air and sunshine do wonders for your spirit.
4. **Listen to your favorite music.** Play a song that makes you smile, brings you peace, or makes you want to dance.
5. **Indulge in simple comforts.** Drink your favorite coffee or tea, light a candle, or wrap yourself in a cozy blanket for a moment of calm.
6. **Call a friend.** You may not have the time or the quiet to have a full conversation, but share a joke or just say hi.

Joy gives us something lovely to hold on to. And these beautiful experiences are gifts from God—glimpses of His grace and love, reminding us that even in difficult and busy seasons, joy is all around.

AFFIRMATION:

I give myself permission to embrace what brings me peace and delight, knowing that God's goodness surrounds me in every season.

81

> Carry each other's burdens, and in this way you will fulfill the law of Christ.
>
> —*Galatians 6:2*

When we stood at the altar, we said "for better or worse" with hope in our hearts. But we had no idea what the future held. Plans change. Expectations get reshaped. The life we imagined stretches to make space for something different, something deeply meaningful—yet undeniably challenging. And in those quiet in-between moments, when no one else sees the sacrifice, we can look at our partner and know we are not doing this alone.

Marriage, when lived out with intention, is less about perfection and more about partnership. A spouse isn't just a partner in bills or parenting logistics. In God's design, they are a teammate. A gift. A reflection of His love when we need it most.

Studies remind us that divorce rates among parents of children with special needs can soar as high as 87 percent.* I reference this statistic not to discourage but rather to highlight the challenges we face. This feels hard because it is.

* Ann Gold Buscho, "Divorce and Special Needs Children," *Psychology Today,* February 28, 2023, www.psychologytoday.com/us/blog/a-better-divorce/202302/divorce-and-special-needs-children/amp.

But through all the various challenges, remember that you're a team. Your spouse was created for you—a partner to walk beside you shoulder to shoulder through life's ups and downs. And when we show up for each other, even in small ways—a quick hug in the hallway, a shared glance of understanding, a whispered prayer before sleep—we are carrying each other's burdens. Together.

AFFIRMATION:

My partner and I are a team, and we stand together through the good and the hard.

82

There are varieties of gifts, but the same Spirit.
—*1 Corinthians 12:4,* ESV

Before I had kids, I thought I knew what the gifts of parenting looked like. I imagined report cards lined with A's, smooth social skills, maybe even trophies and certificates. But raising a child with different abilities has opened my eyes to a fuller, deeper picture of God's creative hand.

Our children, in all their uniqueness, expand our understanding of the world—and of God Himself. Maybe your child is highly sensitive to sound and through them you've learned the sacred power of silence. Maybe their way of seeing the world—through pictures, patterns, or routine—has taught you about order, beauty, and simplicity in ways that words never could. These differences aren't limitations; they are doorways into the richness of God's heart.

I once heard of a child who drew like a printer: meticulously, left to right. It was mesmerizing. It reminded me that there's not one right way to create or express beauty. What the world might view as odd, God may have placed there on purpose—to teach us patience and wonder or to slow us down and make us pay attention.

When we pause to notice how our children move

through life, we see more of God's character—the God who paints outside the lines, who whispers instead of shouts, who created not just one kind of brilliance but *varieties* of gifts, all reflecting His Spirit.

AFFIRMATION:

Through my child, I see more of who God is: creative, intentional, and beautifully diverse.

83

Love your neighbor as yourself.
—*Mark 12:31*

Sometimes the hardest person to love is oneself. As parents, especially ones raising children with special needs, we get in the habit of showing up for everyone else except ourselves. We extend patience, understanding, and grace to others—even strangers. But when it comes to us, we are quick to criticize, slow to forgive, and hesitant to rest.

Mark 12:31 tells us to love our neighbor as ourselves, but what if we're not very kind to ourselves? What if the voice in our head constantly whispers, *You're not doing enough. You should be stronger. You can't afford to slow down.* Those thoughts feel so loud, so familiar, that we begin to believe them. We wear our exhaustion like a badge of honor and feel guilty when we consider taking time for ourselves.

But God never asked us to earn His love through our performance. He sees our efforts, He knows the weight we carry, and He urges us to rest, to receive grace, to live loved.

To love ourselves means to rewire that inner messaging. To replace guilt with grace. To challenge the belief that our worth is tied to how much we do. Self-compassion isn't indulgence; it's obedience to the truth that we are also God's children, deeply worthy of care.

AFFIRMATION:

I release guilt, silence shame, and receive grace. I am worthy of the same compassion I offer to others.

84

Create in me a clean heart, O God,
and renew a right spirit within me.
—*Psalm 51:10*, ESV

There are days when everything feels off: The schedule falls apart, emotions run high, and we feel like we're just barely surviving. It's in these moments that we need to hit the reset button—not just for our day but also for our hearts and minds.

God, in His grace, offers us the opportunity to start fresh. When we feel overwhelmed or defeated, He invites us to come to Him for renewal. Today's verse is a prayer of reset: asking God to realign our spirits with His peace.

Resetting doesn't mean we erase the challenges or forget what happened; it means we pause to take a breath, gain a fresh perspective, and start again.

Take a moment today to reset:

1. **Breathe.** Step away for a minute, close your eyes, and take four deep breaths.
2. **Pray.** Ask God to renew your heart, calm your spirit, and help you move forward with grace.
3. **Let go.** Release what isn't serving you, whether it's guilt, frustration, or the need to control every outcome.

Each reset is a reminder that God's mercies are always fresh, always available. You don't have to be perfect, and your day doesn't have to be flawless to be meaningful. What matters is that you keep going, trusting that God is with you in every minute.

AFFIRMATION:

I give myself permission to reset and lean on God's grace as much as I need to today.

85

Jesus Christ is the same yesterday and today and forever.

—*Hebrews 13:8*

Growing up in church, I'd hear the phrase "Hold to God's unchanging hand." It's a simple truth that has taken on deeper meaning while I raise Maison. When therapies get overwhelming, when progress feels too slow, and when my heart breaks under the weight of exhaustion or worry, God doesn't change; He remains steady, constant, and unshaken.

Picture God's hand reaching out to you, steadying you in the chaos, like a parent guiding their child through a crowded room. His hand is strong, unwavering, and filled with love. You don't need to have it all together; you just need to reach out and hold on.

In the moments that feel unbearable, take a deep breath and whisper a prayer: "Lord, I can't do this without You. Please help me." Seek His peace in your surroundings. Step outside, sit in the quiet, let the warmth of the sun wash over you, or look into the eyes of your loved ones. God's presence can often be felt in the stillness of nature or the simplicity of the moment. His hand is there to hold you, guide you, and give you the strength to keep going. He is constant, unchanging, even in a world that feels so uncertain.

AFFIRMATION:
I hold on to God's unchanging hand, trusting Him to steady me, sustain me, and lead me through each challenge.

86

Before I formed you in the womb I knew you,
before you were born I set you apart;
I appointed you as a prophet to the nations.
—*Jeremiah 1:5*

I was looking into moving Maison from public school to a private school that specializes in autism. One of the schools we were considering asked for a full-scale IQ test as part of their intake process. I didn't think too much of it at the time—I just wanted the best support for my son—so I moved forward with the testing.

But when the results came back, I wasn't prepared for what I read: intellectual disability. My heart sank. I wasn't shocked, because I know my child, but it still stung. I've seen the areas where he struggles to understand things that might come easier to others. Deep down, I had a feeling there was more going on. But still, it hit differently seeing it written on paper.

All day I told myself it was okay—that it didn't change who Maison is. But I wasn't really allowing space for myself to feel. On the drive to pick him up from school, my heart couldn't stand it anymore. I whispered, "God, why? Another thing?" It felt like one more diagnosis on top of everything else. In the car, I let the tears fall, giving myself a moment to just feel it all.

And then the Holy Spirit reminded me of something so tender: "Your eyes saw my unformed body; all the days ordained for me were written in your book before one of them came to be" (Psalm 139:16). That means that every part of Maison's journey was already known and lovingly held by God. I said out loud, "Even with this, Lord, You're still in control. I still trust You with his life."

That truth settled me. It reminded me that God loves Maison even more than I do. I don't need him to be "typical"; I just want him to be happy. And I believe he is and will be, because his story is still being written by the Author of life.

AFFIRMATION:

God wrote every day of my child's life with purpose.
Even this moment is part of His perfect plan.

87

When the cares of my heart are many,
your consolations cheer my soul.
—*Psalm 94:19*, ESV

Anxiety seems like a constant companion sometimes. It shows up when we send our special-needs kids to school, wondering if they'll be safe and understood. It sneaks in during meltdowns, leaving us overwhelmed and unsure of what to do next. It lingers when we entrust our children to others, questioning whether they will receive the care and kindness they deserve.

Anxiety often feels unavoidable, and in many ways, it's a natural response to the unique challenges we face. But we can take steps to manage it, leaning into both practical strategies and God's steadying presence. Rather than ignoring or pretending anxiety isn't present, we push through it while holding on to the peace God offers.

Here are some practical ways to manage anxiety:

1. **Name your feelings.** Anxiety can feel intense, but naming what you're experiencing can help. Pause, breathe, and say, "I feel anxious because . . ." Giving your feelings a name takes away some of their power.
2. **Focus on what you can control.** You can't control every situation that might arise or how others will

treat your child, but you *can* control your preparation and response. Equip yourself with tools, resources, and plans that bring peace of mind.

3. **Create a calming routine.** Develop a routine to ground yourself during anxious moments. This might be a prayer, deep breathing, or reciting scripture that speaks to your heart.
4. **Embrace your support system.** Share your worries with people you trust. A community of understanding friends, family members, and support groups can remind you that you're not alone.
5. **Limit exposure to triggers.** If certain environments or information (such as social media) amplify your anxiety, give yourself permission to step away. Protecting your peace is not avoidance; it's wisdom.
6. **Pray honestly.** Tell God exactly how you're feeling. Pour out your worries to Him, trusting that He hears you and will meet you in your need.

Anxiety may visit often, but it doesn't have to control your days. God sees your fears and the love you have for your child. His peace is with you, in you, and around you.

AFFIRMATION:

Anxiety does not define my days. God's peace is here with me, even in uncertainty.

88

Let your "Yes" be "Yes," and your "No," "No."

—*Matthew 5:37*, NKJV

One afternoon while driving home from work, which seems to be when I find myself in deep thought, I realized that I allow too many people outside my family to dictate my attention. My phone rang all day, and each time I answered, the conversations took away my time and allowed others to load me with emotional weight I wasn't prepared to carry. It all affected my mental health. That day, I decided that I'd no longer grant immediate access to people outside my family. I reminded myself that it was okay to say no and it was okay not to answer someone else's need until I was ready to do so.

Jesus Himself withdrew from the crowds to pray and rest. If the Savior of the world practiced healthy boundaries, how much more should we? Here are a few ways to practice the power of no:

1. **Prioritize your family's needs.** Focus on what's essential for your child, your immediate family, and yourself. All the rest comes second.
2. **Set clear boundaries.** Communicate your limits kindly but firmly. "I can't take this on right now" is a complete sentence.

3. **Trust God's provision.** Let go of things that don't serve your well-being. Saying no doesn't mean you're letting others down. Trust that God will provide help from other sources when you can't step in.
4. **Celebrate your yeses.** When you say no to things that drain you, you're saying yes to your family's peace and joy and the work God is calling you to do. Allow yourself to focus on and enjoy those things.

Saying no allows you to steward your limits, time, energy, and peace. Each no creates space for the yeses that matter most.

AFFIRMATION:

I release the guilt of saying no and embrace healthy boundaries. My yeses will align with what God has called me to prioritize.

89

The LORD makes firm the steps
of the one who delights in him;
though he may stumble, he will not fall,
for the LORD upholds him with his hand.
—*Psalm 37:23–24*

Parenting a child with special needs is not a race to the finish line or a marathon to endure. It's a journey—one filled with winding paths, unexpected detours, and breathtaking views of God's grace along the way.

In our fast-paced world, it's easy to feel as though we're constantly falling behind. Progress can seem slow, milestones come at their own pace, and comparison with other families can confuse our way. But here's the truth: God didn't design this journey to be about speed or a destination. He designed it to be an experience of trust, growth, and the beauty found with every step.

The world may measure success by how far and how fast we go, but God celebrates each step we take. That first word spoken, that moment of connection, even those days when all we can do is keep going—these are all victories. They are reminders that the journey is sacred, no matter the pace.

Think of how the Lord establishes our steps, even

when we can't see the entire road ahead. Like a gentle guide, He walks with us, offering strength when we are weak and peace when the path feels overwhelming. In His presence, we are reminded that the journey is not a test or a race. The journey is a walk of faith, where we learn to trust Him more deeply with every step.

Take a moment today to pause and breathe. Celebrate the path you've walked, your own unique story. Reflect on the ways God has walked with you, carried you, and provided for your family.

AFFIRMATION:

I release the pressure to race ahead, and I embrace the beauty of this journey.

90

> Be strong and courageous. Do not be afraid; do not be discouraged, for the LORD your God will be with you wherever you go.
>
> —*Joshua 1:9*

This verse is a rallying cry. It's God's encouragement to us to keep moving forward—not because we have all the answers but because we know the One who does. When the road feels long and your strength feels small, remember that you are not walking it alone.

Take a moment to reset your posture—both physically and spiritually. Remind yourself of who you are: a resilient, loving parent chosen by God to nurture and advocate for your child. And no bad day, no mistake, no critical comment can change who you are. Stand tall in your calling. As you start your day, speak words of life and encouragement to yourself. Say them aloud even. Tell yourself, "I am capable. I am strong. I am loved. I am courageous." And when anxiety creeps in, pause and ground yourself. Breathe deeply and remember God's promise that He is with you.

And no matter how minor, take time to celebrate victories in your day. These moments remind you of progress, even in the midst of struggle.

God sees you, loves you, and equips you to keep going, so lift your head up! Keep your eyes on Him and stay encouraged because the Lord of all is walking beside you every step of the way.

AFFIRMATION:

I am strong and courageous, and God is by my side.

ABOUT THE AUTHOR

CAMILLE JOY is a passionate advocate, storyteller, and beacon of hope for families raising children with special needs. She is the founder of the Ausomely Different Foundation, a nonprofit dedicated to supporting families of children with autism and other developmental disabilities through life-saving resources, advocacy, and inclusive community events. Camille is also the host of the globally recognized *Moments of Joy* podcast and the creator of Moments of Joy Fest, an annual celebration that brings together families from around the world.

As a devoted wife and mother of five, including a son with autism and congenital heart disease, Camille draws from her own journey to empower and uplift other parents. Her work has been featured on major platforms like ABC News, where she was highlighted for championing sensory-friendly movie screenings. She also serves as co-director of the documentary *Parents of the Spectrum,* a powerful film that amplifies the voices of families raising children with autism. Through her storytelling, public speaking, and media platforms, Camille creates space for honest conversations, healing, and joy, offering encouragement, education, and the message that families are never alone.